HONEY

OLDER WOMEN

Each farmer on the island conceals
his hive far up on the mountain,
knowing it will otherwise be plundered.
When they die, or can no longer make
the hard climb, the lost combs
year after year grow heavier with honey.
And the sweetness has more and more
acutely the taste of that wilderness.

Jack Gilbert: The Great Fires—Poems 1982-1992

HONEY

A CONNOISSEUR'S GUIDE
WITH RECIPES

GENE OPTON

RECIPES BY GENE OPTON
AND NANCIE HUGHES

TEN SPEED PRESS
Berkeley Toronto

ACKNOWLEDGEMENTS

So many people have served to enrich my understanding of honey that I cannot name them all, but I would like to acknowledge the invaluable contributions of the International Bee Research Association in Cardiff, Wales; the National Honey Board; my publisher at Ten Speed Press, Phil Wood, and my editor, Julie Bennett; my honey team in Paris, led by Jean Michel Nowak; the spirit of Catherine Brandel; friends whose comments improved the text; and, most of all, beekeepers all over the country for their generous reports of their experience.

Ten Speed Press
PO Box 7123, Berkeley, California 94707
www.tenspeed.com

Distributed in Australia by Simon & Schuster Australia, in Canada by Ten Speed Press Canada, in New Zealand by Southern Publishers Group, in South Africa by Real Books, in Southeast Asia by Berkeley Books, and in the United Kingdom and Europe by Airlift Books.

The poem "Older Women" (page ii) is from *The Great Fires—Poems 1982–1992* by Jack Gilbert. Copyright © 1994 by Jack Gilbert. Reprinted by permission of Alfred A. Knopf, a division of Random House, Inc.

Permission to use the watercolor image of the apiary at Luxembourg Gardens (page vi) courtesy of the artist, Philippe Dequesne, and La Société Centrale d'Apiculture in Paris, France.

Cover and interior design by Jamison Design
Food Photography by Joyce Oudkerk Pool
Food Styling by Pouké

Additional photography credits:
Honey display at the Minnesota State Fair
 (page 6) courtesy of Winnie Johnson.
Honeycomb and honey extractors (pages 3, 5, and 7)
 courtesy of the National Honey Board.
Beekeepers and honey jars at Luxembourg Gardens
 (pages 2 and 11) courtesy of Jean-Pascal Roux.
Apiary sign, single hive and four hives at Luxembourg
Gardens (pages 1, 10, and 11) courtesy of Claudia Koch.

Library of Congress Cataloging-in-Publication Data
Opton, Gene.
  Honey : a connoisseur's guide with recipes /
  Gene Opton ; recipes by Gene Opton and Nancie
Hughes.
    p. cm.
  ISBN 1-58008-177-0 (pbk.)
  1. Cookery (Honey) I. Hughes, Nancie. II. Title.

TX767.H7 O668 2000
641.6'8—dc21
                                        99-054700

Some of this material originally appeared in *Honey Feast: A Sampler of Honey Recipes* by Gene Opton and Nancie Hughes, copyright © 1975 by Gene Opton, published by Apple Pie Press/Ten Speed Press, Berkeley, CA.

First printing, 2000.
Printed in Hong Kong

1 2 3 4 5 6 7 8 9 10 — 04 03 02 01 00

CONTENTS

An Introduction to Honey

Jars of honey—hex shaped, bear shaped, skep shaped, with squeeze lids or embossed with decorative bees—cover my kitchen counter. Small spoons sit in a glass ready to use for tasting. To my visitors, I suggest combinations that demonstrate the variety of flavors in honey. I find myself describing the plants that are nectar sources for the bees, and how it is possible to know that a honey is actually made from one specific flower, say, the New Jersey blueberry. And what you can learn from reading a label, and what you need to know about the way packers treat honey before it goes into the jar.

I can carry on at length about honey. I marvel at the timing of a season in which rainfall and sun and open blossoms must be in the right state at the right time to allow the collecting of nectar, and at the bees, who act with such intricate cooperation that the colony is sometimes called a superorganism. I marvel that it has been on earth for 20 million years or more, probably hunted by humankind since they appeared on earth. Ancient Egyptians sacrificed honey by the ton to their river gods. Roman legions slathered honey on wounds to promote healing. Medieval lords reserved honey for their private use, and cloistered beekeepers took the wax of supposed virgin bees to make sacramental candles. By the sixteenth century a Spanish naturalist correctly identified the head of the hive (recognized since ancient times as a hierarchy) as a female, with her paramount assignment the prodigious laying of eggs.

Honey is found everywhere today, from farmstands to supermarkets, made by bees on unpeopled plains and on the rooftops of our largest cities. Honey is so complex in nature that it invites people to examine it as they do wine, to savor each nuance of flavor and the circumstances that led to its production, appreciating the singular personality of each kind of honey, ultimately searching out the rare and sublime.

Soil, plants, weather, and the bee population act in an unpredictable conjunction that allows the bees to take in nectar (minute drops of liquid to which they add their own enzymes and body heat), and elaborate it into a supersaturated solution of fructose, glucose, and some water along with small components of vitamins, minerals, ash, and protein. The honey then nourishes other workers and brood, the next generation of bees, their numbers so carefully sized that the colony is largest when work must be done and smallest for the dearth time of winter. Bees have a good sense, then, of issues as great as population control. The beekeeper's job is to see that the bees are content.

My book *Honey Feast*, an earlier version of this book, was published twenty-five years ago, with recipes from a variety of cultures, some reflecting the use of honey in traditions many hundreds of years old. Nancie Hughes and I were kept so busy researching and testing recipes, we didn't even attempt to describe where honey comes from. Now I find myself immersed in accounts of life in the hive, by the long historical record on bees and honey, by stories beekeepers tell about their work. I am immersed in tasting and comparing honeys gathered from sources all over the country and the world. I scout out honeys I have read about, sample crimped-paper cupfuls of locally produced honey at tented tables at the farmers' market, or quickly send off an order when a long-sought kind of honey appears on the list of a shop in Michigan. I take time to appreciate honey.

Over the years, alfalfa honey has become my standard table honey—its slightly viscous texture seems to go with everything, and its full, rounded flavor (not too sweet) satisfies my personal taste as a topping for yogurt or the occasional batch of hot biscuits. The alfalfa honey I buy, which was collected from hives in the foothills of the Sierra Nevadas in central California, is sold in several stores in Berkeley under the label of the Mendocino Honey Company. Rolla Ogle, the packager who signs each jar, is not himself a beekeeper. He handles the harvests of several beekeepers around the state who send their honey in fifty-gallon barrels to his packaging station in Potter Valley.

To prepare the honey for distribution into stores, Ogle transfers the contents of a barrel into five-gallon pails that are set in a hot-water bath overnight. On the next day, the honey, liquefied by gentle heat, is gravity-fed through a cloth filter into standard-issue heatproof canning jars. With the help of a machine that applies the glue, Ogle hand labels each jar. He uses water-soluble glue, allowing consumers to reuse the jars for their own pickling projects.

In a year, Ogle packages the yield from 500 to 600 hives, amounting to about 125,000 pounds. Six beekeepers whom he works with follow the blossoms, moving their hives as the season progresses. One beekeeper in the north central California town of Yreka takes his bees to the great expanses of flowering fields in North Dakota for the summer. A Minnesota beekeeper takes his hives to Texas for the winter. Clover honey comes from Alberta, Canada, over toward the Peace River.

There are large packers of honey in America (only fifteen companies supply more than half of the honey for sale nationwide), there are small ones like Ogle, and there are many sizes in between. Beekeepers manage the hives, siting them for a good honey yield, seeing to the bees' needs, harvesting the combs, and sometimes completing the packaging process. The actual processing of the honey is done only by the bees themselves.

Small packagers can give more attention to retaining the natural substances in honey, devising gentler methods for liquefying. One Oregon beekeeper sets buckets of honey in a baker's proofing cabinet designed to raise bread dough at a uniform 100 degrees. Another has converted a refrigerator into a warmer. Beekeepers unwilling to warm a honey sufficiently to flow through a very fine filter may use just a strainer. Pollen, propolis particles, bits of bee legs and wings, and chunks of comb that float to the surface in the holding tubs can be skimmed off. Bits that make their way into the jars are edible, however, and some people even welcome them for extra health value. Honey may be labelled "raw," although there is no uniform code on using this term. Using as little heat as possible is a sign of careful handling.

Comb honey is one way to experience honey as it comes from the hive, with no further handling at all. Beeswax comb is completely edible and has a supple texture to the tooth. Comb honey is sometimes available in 3½-inch plastic rounds that began as open-ended sleeves in the upper part of the hive, lined with a thin foundation of comb for the bees to build on. Once the little rounds are filled, they are fitted with a bottom and a top, and the honey is actually untouched by human hands before it goes to market. Another form of comb honey is made by bees in 4-inch square wood frames. Cut comb honey is sold in two forms—one where harvested large comb is cut into sections and fitted into boxes, and another where pieces of cut comb are inserted into jars of liquid honey.

Another form of honey is made by a carefully managed process of crystallization that creates very fine crystals, producing an unctuous spread termed "creamed" or "spun" or "creme" honey. The crystallization process lightens the color of a honey. Premium creamed lavender honey from the south of France is white in the jar.

Crystallization is easily reversible. Place a container of honey, lid removed, in a pan of hot water (about 140 degrees, which is less than boiling temperature) and let it stand until it liquefies. Because honey re-crystallizes, you may want to liquefy only the amount that you will use up in a few days' time. You can put grainy honey on hot oatmeal or toast, and the granules will melt as you eat.

Who can guess why this bee-tailored food appeals so strongly to humans? But men have been ready to risk painful beestings in order to harvest honey for thousands of years. Our earliest record, painted into a cave in eastern Spain about 6000 B.C., shows a climber in pursuit of honey hanging high in a tree in the face of defending bees.

VISITING A BEE AND HONEY HALL

On the last day of August, I visited the Minnesota State Fair. One petal-shaped wing of the Agriculture and Horticulture building was identified in faded paint. It read "Bee and Honey."

When I walked in with my sister, we were immediately confronted by a demonstration of honey harvesting staged near the entrance. A man wearing thin surgical gloves rested a full honeycomb on the edge of a three-foot-tall stainless steel bowl. He passed a broad knife along the comb, removing in thin wrinkled sheets the topmost cap of wax covering the honey-filled cells. The hot knife was not warmed today because no electrical outlet could be found, but this twenty-five-year veteran beekeeper removed the wax cap with a few confident strokes, the wooden sides of the frame acting as a guide to the knife. Then

he sliced off the cap on the other side so the honey could spill freely from both directions. Six opened combs had already been placed in the extractor, and now this fresh one was placed perpendicular to the sides of the bowl. The man gripped a knob-like handle and set the huge bowl spinning, centrifuge action splashing the honey onto the sides of the bowl. In moments, a stream of honey issued from a spout near the bottom of the vat, passing through a metal strainer into a large collecting jar. A few bits of comb tumbled out, to be caught by the strainer. Honey flowed into the jar, its level rising as the extractor whirled on.

We continued exploring the honey hall. Rounding a curve, we stopped suddenly in awe. In the center of the room a structure displayed honey in jars, their light-drenched colors ranging from almost clear to rich dark brown. I had never seen so much honey, or such a complete spectrum. Each row from top to bottom displayed perfectly color-matched jars, starting with the palest (called "water white" in the trade) and shading into

amber and medium amber tones, curving around through the dark amber range and ending with the near-black tones of Minnesota buckwheat honey.

A guardrail kept us at a distance from the panorama of glowing jars. In a walkway between the rail and the display racks sat an upright rectangle of clear Plexiglas holding a cross section of a hive with hundreds of live bees working on comb. Most of the bees were in the lower two-thirds of the comb, which contained the brood nest; they moved across the surface and in and out of empty cells around the edges. Some of the bees made sweeping motions with their legs, indicating that they may have been cleaning out a cell vacated by an emerging bee, making it ready to receive another egg. Some cells of the comb were opaque with yellow plugs of pollen, a protein source fed to developing bees along with their ration of honey. Around the pollen stores were the brood cells containing eggs, larvae, or pupae, recognized by the purposeful actions of bees who ducked in and rapidly retreated after conveying morsels to the young. Pupae enclosed in cells secrete a pheromone that attracts workers, whose bodies clustering on the surface of the comb maintain the temperature needed by the pupae to develop into mature insects.

Bees clumped together around one slower-moving bee who was marked with a bit of white paint—the queen. Although a beekeeper could probably spot the queen because she is larger than the others (with a longer and wider abdomen and longer legs), I was grateful for the painted clue. With small deft movements of her forelegs, this Minnesota queen felt her way into cells as she moved along, inserting eggs into empty chambers. Her escorts of attendant bees supply her with snacks, groom her constantly, and at the same time acquire chemical signals from her that regulate their behavior. She may move somewhat slower than a worker bee, but in a single day the queen can lay her own weight in eggs, as many as one thousand eggs. In the three years that she lives she may produce half a million eggs.

The upper section of this display, smaller in size, housed luminous comb filled only with honey. In a large hive, the queen is kept out of the top layers by a grid (queen excluder), sized to allow only the smaller worker bees to pass through. Since eggs are not laid in this comb, honey can be harvested without destroying any of the colony's young. Here bees bustled along the surface of the comb, depositing miniscule drops of nectar into open cells or daubing full cells with bits of wax until a covering cap was complete. They reuse old wax, or young bees make fresh beeswax from glands in their abdomen.

Typical hive structures were displayed around the honey hall. Inside the hives, sets of framed combs were suspended on runners, like the files in a suspension filing system. All dimensions of the hives are precisely engineered to accommodate the bees' activity. Until the middle of the nineteenth century, honey could be harvested only with considerable disturbance of the bees and inadvertent destruction of brood chambers. Then a beekeeper in Philadelphia figured out that if you separate all the parts of the hive by the distance of a "bee space" (an opening less than half an inch, just large enough to allow bees to move freely through it but not so small that it excites them to build comb across it), you can freely lift out the upper combs without affecting the vigor of the colony. Moveable-frame hives of this sort have become the basis of today's honey industry.

We learned from a guide that a hive kept to winter in Minnesota has to be left with eighty-five pounds of honey to carry the bee colony through. We learned that an entomologist at the university is working on a strain of bees that can overcome a plague of parasitic mites, which in spreading across the country in recent years threatens beekeeping operations of all sizes. We learned that of all the offerings at the state fair concession stands, none tasted better than freshly made honey ice cream eaten on the grass outside the Agricultural Hall on this warm summer day.

Honey is the rare, perhaps only, foodstuff that needs no additives to give it a long shelf life. When bees elaborate nectar into honey, their main objective may be to create a substance resistant to spoilage to supply them with energy and food in dearth times to come. Their success is so complete that honey found in ancient Egyptian tombs was edible. Still, honey flavor is at its peak shortly after harvest, and some experts now recommend storing honey in the freezer, very tightly wrapped, to retain the best flavor.

The soothing effect of honey for easing coughs and sore throats is so widely appreciated that a buyer for specialty foodstores in my community makes a practice of stocking locally produced honey in winter, during the time of colds and flu, when it may also strengthen the immune system.

Honey is widely used as a quick source of energy, becoming a staple ingredient of the ubiquitous energy bars. It is easily digested because its main sugars, fructose and glucose, are absorbed directly into the blood. This also means that honey is absorbed by the body with less effect on blood glucose levels than sugar, which is chiefly sucrose. The primary nutritional value of honey is as a provider of carbohydrates, yielding approximately sixty calories per tablespoon.

The beneficial effects of honey and hive products are often talked about, although scientific knowledge is only slowly being accumulated. A beekeeper in the Midwest reported that she cured her own hay fever with locally made honey. Many of the people I meet at our farmers' market rely on local honey for relief of their allergy symptoms. A Hawaiian beekeeper who burned the side of his face told me that honey applied to his burns tightened the welts down miraculously. When he uses honey on the cuts and scratches he gets repairing hives, the wounds heal quickly. Sue Hubbell, author of *A Book of Bees* and a commercial beekeeper, found that beestings relieved her arthritic hands. A New Mexico beekeeper told me that his bothersome, X-ray-confirmed arthritis went away when he returned to beekeeping and has not reappeared in seventeen years. Most beekeepers, I've often been told, don't get arthritis.

The ancient Egyptians, Greeks, Romans, and Asians used dressings of honey mixed with fat as a treatment for wounds. Honey was used as a preservative in embalming; for instance, the body of Alexander the Great was embalmed with honey. Medicines used from ancient times and through the Middle Ages included honey in their formulas. Honey continues to be used as a surgical dressing in some modern hospitals, and as a medium for storing skin grafts and corneas.

Honey's effectiveness for applications of this sort stems from its character as an antimicrobial agent, due in part to its hygroscopic character. Honey over a wound or burn absorbs water and body fluids, desiccating bacteria and fungi and inhibiting their growth. Honey's natural acidity also contributes to its antimicrobial effect.

For medicinal use, the preferred type of honey is that which has been extracted from the comb with minimal processing. Heating and processing destroy some active enzymes, vitamins, and volatile constituents in the honey, as well as those in any pollen and propolis that may be present.

Health and medicinal uses of hive products apart from honey are being explored around the world as a result of modern production capabilities. Royal jelly, the enriched carbohydrate that, fed to larvae, converts them to new queens, is particularly prized in Asia. Propolis, sticky substances that the bees collect from tree resins and use to seal together parts of the hive, is an antiseptic that does not spoil. Both pollen and propolis are widely sold in ointments and capsules. Special farming techniques produce a supply of bee venom. Researchers in Holland expect to produce a test batch of medicinal petunia honey in the year 2000 made from petunias whose genes have been altered to yield medically useful proteins.

About a third of the world's food crops for human consumption are pollinated by bees. Profits from the crops greatly exceed the profit from the honey produced. Considering the great chain of effort that goes into creating harvestable honey, the total output is small enough to rank honey as a luxury product, as it has been throughout human history. While bees and food crops share an interdependency that is essential to the well-being of our species, care and attention to bee colonies pay off by providing not only a prized sweet but also essential benefits to our food supply.

People who have observed the activities of country life anywhere are imprinted forever with images of bees, flowers, and fields. Who could forget the sight of beekeepers in Provence ladling honey into hives in the spring, nourishing the bees into readiness for the onset of the nectar flow? When the blossoms of a crop are about to reach their peak, the French farmers communicate back and forth with beekeepers, who are ready to move their hives at night when the bees are quiet. Come morning the bees put themselves to work collecting nectar from fields of blossoming zucchini or blooming apple trees, pollinating all the while.

More than 17 million bees call Paris home. However, none of the urban bee colonies are more elegantly housed than those who reside in the jardin du Luxembourg in Paris's sixth arrondissement, their hives capped by peaked roofs to match the angles of the gazebo they are clustered around. This pristine apiary has existed since the 1870s, not only creating a great show of flowers through the bees' achievements in pollinating, but also as a teaching facility for future beekeepers. Since 1991 the program has focused on people who want to produce honey in the center of the city, where the bees draw on the established stands of acacias, linden trees, and chestnuts in the gardens at the Tuilleries and the Palais-Royal as well as the diverse plants of private gardens.

Parisians who are not eager to take the hands-on approach can buy honey at the once-a-year sale held in autumn. Hundreds queue up for the opportunity to carry home plastic pails with the distinctive label of the Rucher du Luxembourg, honey that comes in several shades of amber depending on the season when it was harvested. On sale days the head beekeeper, his white jacket resembling a chef's coat, stages a demonstration outdoors in the gazebo. He lifts honeycomb from a hive after the bees have been subdued by smoke, and describes the process of honey gathering to a circle of interested listeners. The bees' pavilion, complete with a hex-shaped pool to provide water, can be visited during all the hours the park is open, and the quiet hum of the

hives on a warm afternoon underscores the pleasure of viewing the meticulously groomed lawns, flower beds, and sculpted hedges of this formally conceived garden.

The Flavors of Honey

That we are able to obtain single-flower honeys at all results from the conjunction of the bee's habits and the watchful effort of harvesting beekeepers.

GATHERING THE NECTAR

Bees who have gathered nectar from a certain flower choose to return to another flower of the same sort; they communicate to other foragers in the hive, by means of scent and physical movement, the location of the specific nectar source. Aristotle reported this behavior in the third century B.C., and it matches modern observation: "On each expedition the bee does not fly from a flower of one kind to a flower of another, but flies from one violet, say, to another violet, and never meddles with another flower until it has got back to the hive; on reaching the hive they throw off their load, and each bee on her return is followed by three or four companions."

Bees can select the best-yielding nectar source available at a given time, which leads them to concentrate on a single source. Hives that have been moved into blooming fields for purposes of pollination offer bees a great single source to collect from.

Once the nectar has been carried in and the bees have set to work converting it to honey, a beekeeper who wants to keep the harvest separate will pull off the topmost layers of the hive as soon as the bees have capped the honey cells and before they bring in the nectar of subsequent crops. Beekeepers can judge if they have a single source by a uniform color in the comb.

THE BEST KIND OF BEE

For hundreds of years beekeepers have favored European races of the honeybee species, Apis mellifera, for their hives. Desirable attributes in these bees include a "gentle" personality—they are amenable to management, they tend to stay on the comb when the hive is worked on, they are slow to alarm or to swarm, and they make copious amounts of honey. By the 1800s, these bees had been introduced to all the major honey-producing parts of the world, including Hawaii and New Zealand.

Since the life span of a bee is just weeks or months, the population of a colony is in a state of constant renewal. The effects of interbreeding are quickly seen. With the idea of improving bloodlines, queen bees of a tropical African race were imported to Piracicaba, Brazil, in 1956. The progeny of forty-nine of those queens have since spread across South and Central America into the United States, frequently supplanting European bees.

The interbred Africanized ("killer") bees are not satisfactory honey providers, and they sting humans and animals viciously because of a fast-trigger alarm response that also summons large numbers of bees to the attack. In 1999, a Los Angeles man who was mowing his lawn was stung to death by feral Africanized bees that had settled in adjacent abandoned beehives.

The Africanized bees are so successful at interbreeding that they pose a threat to existing bee colonies as well as to humans and animals. Africanized bees set up colonies in smaller spaces, swarm frequently, and have adapted to a wide range of environments, allowing them to extend their territory. At the same time, they do not establish stores of honey that are available for human harvesting, and they exact a severe price from honey collectors with their stings. Beekeepers can monitor the populations of their hives and introduce a replacement queen if they observe irregular behavior by the bees.

Bees forage within a one-mile radius of the hive and may well contribute nectar from some other choice blossoms within their range, but small additions do not significantly alter the impact of the major source. The United States Department of Agriculture (USDA) requires that, in order to be labeled as a certain variety, a honey must be eighty percent from the named source. A beekeeper may know that a certain varietal dominates his or her harvest to an even greater degree. A New Mexico beekeeper, moving his hives at peak bloom time into a 120-acre stand of white clover that has been pushed to heights of six feet by an abundance of late rainfall, is pretty sure that his honey will be ninety-nine percent clover.

In some areas of the country, one bloom time follows another so closely that it is virtually impossible to separate them—in the Midwest, for example, tulip poplars bloom right after the acacia trees, and apple trees bloom with the earliest spring flowers. In Oregon, cherries and maples flower at the same time. The combs, filled with what the bees had available, will yield a blended honey. In the fall, when the great surges of spring blossoms have ended, bees must rely on a wider range of nectar sources, and late-gathered honey is usually from assorted sources and darker in color than early harvests.

Honey collected by bees from several sources is usually called "mixed flower" or "wildflower." Among the smaller honey producers, plants that are likely to have contributed to a certain batch of wildflower honey may very well be known, because the producers know what is in bloom in the locale they collect from. One jar of dark honey labeled wildflower was actually bamboo, I was told, because the hives that year had been moved down along the Ohio River where only bamboo would have been available to the bees.

Another kind of blending occurs when beekeepers, in order to make up the fifty-gallon barrels that are standard in the trade, combine the harvests from different hives. Very large packers of honey may mix together honey from different sources, even including imported ones, to make a product that conforms in color and taste to the accepted characteristics of a specific varietal such as clover.

The flavor of each honey depends on the nectar source. Nectar itself is composed mainly of sucrose and water. Bees add enzymes that create additional chemical compounds, inverting the sucrose into fructose and glucose, and they evaporate water so that the resulting product (less than eighteen percent water) will resist spoiling. As many as nineteen organic acids are found in honey, although only some of them will occur in any given honey. Exactly what creates the finished flavor has not yet been sorted out.

Some of the substances that give honey aroma and flavor occur in all honeys, and other substances occur only in the honey made from specific plants. A few honeys are markedly different: heather, manuka, and buckwheat are higher in protein, which probably affects their flavor as well as their higher level of antimicrobial properties. Certain amino acids may cause a bitter flavor; tannins add a flavor that some people find unpleasant.

While nectar is the bees' most abundant source for honey, bees also make honey from honeydew, an insect-processed material derived from the sap of certain trees. Honey from conifers—which is made entirely from honeydew—tends to be dark in color with a relatively high mineral content.

Even if the reasons behind the unique flavor of each varietal are not scientifically explained, the flavors themselves are well known and recognizable and some have become familiar. As specialty stores and farmers' markets supplement the larger distribution centers, people can explore new choices and discover new preferences. A Midwestern beekeeper told me she had trouble persuading her customers to buy goldenrod honey from a fine harvest one autumn, despite its enticing yellow color, perhaps because of the old knock against goldenrod, which for years was said to cause hay fever (which it doesn't). People who actually tasted her goldenrod honey bought it enthusiastically. Sunflower honey flew off the shelves after a recent study pointed out that antioxidants in honey vary greatly depending on the nectar source, with sunflower and buckwheat at the top of the list. The limited supply of tupelo honey, which comes only from a very small area of Florida swampland, was barely equal to national demand after it made an appearance in a popular film.

HOW TO TASTE HONEY

My friend Jean Michel, freshly arrived in Berkeley from Paris, leaves a jar on the little table just outside my kitchen door. The flowing liquid inside is pale golden except for a cream-colored cloudlike mass that looks rather like the embryo in an egg white, all wispy edges, suspended near the top of the jar. When I pick up the jar the next morning, its contents have turned into a uniform, cloudy, pale-gold solid. I scrape a portion of the soft mass with my thumb to taste it.

This honey tastes mild but complex; my tongue notices fine grains in the mixture. In the cool hours of the night, the small "seed" of granules I noticed at first has acted to convert all the liquid into a granulated state, still soft enough to be spreadable. In these few hours the process of granulation has occurred, a change that occurs naturally in honey, especially in the ones that are high in glucose. Perhaps the transatlantic flight has speeded up the molecules in this sample gathered in the vicinity of l'Opéra in Paris. Some enterprising beekeeper has set up hives and is collecting enough honey, right in the middle of urban Paris, to offer it for sale at the gift shop of the opera house.

That cloudy jar of crystallized honey is no cause for concern. Honey is edible straight from the hive; it needs no additives to preserve it, and it will, by natural process, crystallize, whether it does so in weeks, months, or years after harvest. A few honeys—tupelo is one—tend to stay liquid, whereas some honeys, like lavender, rush to crystallize. Honey that has been heated to 130 or 140 degrees will remain liquid for a few months. Passing the honey through a filter that removes pollen and other bits that can act as the nuclei of crystals also postpones the crystallization process. Packers are under pressure to provide American consumers with liquid honey because that is what moves most readily from supermarket shelves.

A garden at different times of day contains a moving pattern of fragrance, for the sun warms one part and then another, bringing out the aroma of first this plant and then its neighbors. Oreganos and thymes that are bland in the cool of morning emit a powerful perfume in the heat of the afternoon sun.

The range of flavors in honey is just as complex. Exploring the taste of a honey takes only a little time and attention. Take a moment before tasting to notice the aroma of the honey in the jar. Then spoon out a dollop of honey, less than an eighth of a teaspoon. Put it in your mouth, and allow it to dissolve on the front of your tongue.

Your tastebuds respond as the honey dissolves. You may smack your lips to sort out the full range of flavor. As the honey flows to the back and sides of your mouth, later-developing flavors appear. You may observe a lingering aftertaste.

When you taste several honeys in a row, try drinking hot black tea in between to keep the palate clear. Unsalted crackers can restore your tasting apparatus. Give your mouth time to sort out individual complexities before moving on to another sample.

In a tasting for professional chefs, the National Honey Advisory Board provided fireweed and clover (light in color), eucalyptus and orange blossom (golden), blueberry (amber), and buckwheat (dark amber). Fireweed has its own way of being sweet and complex at the same time. Clover has that classic honey taste. Eucalyptus is rich and full, and orange blossom is more perfumed with a sweeter quality. Blueberry honey, complex and aromatic, leaves a blueberry aftertaste; buckwheat is strong and tangy.

You can set up a taste comparison of several honeys simply by selecting honeys of different colors. A general rule is that light honey is mild in flavor, golden is richer, and dark honey can be strong-flavored. You could choose light clover honey and golden alfalfa or sage, plus a dark one—a wildflower mix, or buckwheat or chestnut. Keep each taste small, so that the fundamental sweetness does not overwhelm the other flavor components.

Include a creamed honey and notice how taste is altered by your response to the difference in texture. Include comb honey for another effect.

You may want to arrange tastings with more specific goals. A few combinations are suggested below. You will discover many more possibilities by consulting the tasting notes that follow.

Tasting Combinations

FROM MILD TO STRONG FLAVORS:
- Acacia
- Lemon
- Alfalfa
- Buckwheat

NATURALLY CRYSTAL-LIZED HONEYS FROM A VARIETY OF NECTARS:
- Hawaiian White
- French Lavender
- Italian Lime
- Florida Orange Blossom

THREE TOTALLY DIFFERENT FLAVORS:
- Acacia or Clover
- Raspberry
- Buckwheat

TWO FLORAL, TWO HERBAL BOUQUETS:
- Clover
- Tupelo
- Sage
- Thyme

STRIKING CONTRASTS —A FLOWER, AN HERB, TWO TREES:
- Leatherwood
- Lavender
- Pine
- Chestnut

VARIETAL HONEY TASTING NOTES

Each of the following honeys was tasted in my Berkeley kitchen. I have reported on the color, texture, and flavors as they appeared to me. My collection of honey came from farmers' markets, local shops, and catalogs. Some of my favorites are the work of artisan producers—small suppliers who take a personal interest in all aspects of their product, harvesting only in specifically designated areas and using little heat or filtering when transferring honey to the jar. Some honeys so captivated me that I gave them special designations:

SILVER SPOON SELECTION:
Honey with a flavor so nuanced that it is best appreciated in tiny discrete amounts. Honey that you would choose to eat from a spoon.

CONNOISSEUR SELECTION:
Honey with a distinctive flavor, of interest to the most sophisticated palate, representing a particular dimension in the range of flavor possibilities.

ACACIA (*Italy; France*). Very light in color (white); smooth liquid. Exquisite delicate flavor free of cloying aftertaste. Excellent for baking as well as eating. Silver spoon selection. See also black locust.

ALFALFA (*United States; Canada*). Medium amber, flowing. Mild and full flavor makes it an excellent table honey. Widely available.

 AVOCADO (*California*). Dark amber, flowing. Richly flavored with a floral bouquet; milder flavor than its color would suggest. Good table honey.

BASSWOOD (*United States*). Very light color, flowing. Distinctive biting flavor. Nectar source: basswood trees with cream-colored flowers that bloom in late June and July from southern Canada to Alabama to Texas. Widely available throughout eastern United States.

BLACK LOCUST (*United States*). Water white color, flowing. Mild, sweet, and pure. One extremely light, greenish gold sample suggested honeydew melon. High fructose content, slow to granulate. Nectar source: *Robinia pseudoacacia* native to North America. May bloom so early in spring that nectar is limited by late-occurring rainfall.

BLACKBERRY (*United States*). Amber, flowing. Rich, zesty flavor with tones of the black-berry fruit that are also evident in its aroma. The berry flavor is enhanced when it is eaten with plain yogurt. Nectar source: pollination of blackberry crops in Washington and Oregon. Excellent table honey.

BLUEBERRY (*United States*). Amber, flowing. Broad, pleasant flavor, with a slight tang and a blueberry aftertaste. The berry flavor enhanced by eating it on plain yogurt. Beekeepers say the honey tastes the way blueberry blossoms smell. Nectar source: tiny white flowers of blueberry shrubs of farmers in Florida, Michigan, New Jersey, and Oregon; the honey is a bonus from bees used as pollinators for the blueberry crop. Good table honey.

BUCKWHEAT (*United States*). Dark amber, flowing. Bold, distinctive flavor that varies widely according to source. Can be substituted for molasses. Recent studies examining different floral sources have found a high antioxidant quality in buckwheat honey. Widely available.

CHESTNUT (*Italy; France*). Dark amber, flowing. Distinctive, smooth, complex, nutty, clean flavor; not sweet. Excellent for use as a condiment, drizzled on a simple white cheese or over roasted figs.

CHRISTMAS BERRY (*Hawaii*). Medium amber, partly crystallized. Distinctive, rich light flavor suggests papaya.

CLOVER (*United States; Canada*). Light golden, flowing. Sweet, mild, rounded flavor. White clover in particular, grown as a widespread perennial pasture crop, is a major nectar source in many parts of the world. Alsike clover, crimson clover, red clover, and sweet clover are also great honey resources. Excellent for baking as well as eating. Widely available.

CRANBERRY (*Wisconsin; Oregon*). Medium amber, flowing. Intense flavor includes elements that are puckery, almost bitter. The berry quality is enhanced by eating it with plain yogurt. Nectar source: intensive honeybee pollination of cranberry bogs.

EUCALYPTUS (*United States*). Golden, flowing. Genus *Eucalyptus* is very large and honeys vary greatly in color and flavor. Tends to be bold, but not as pungent as expected knowing the powerful fragrance of the trees. Mellow, with a hint of menthol. Widely available.

FIR TREE (*France*). Dark amber, free flowing. Hints of resin and menthol in its strong, distinctive flavor; palate cleansing.

FIREWEED (*Washington state*). Light gold, flowing. Mild, spicy flavor. Nectar source: pink flowers of the plants that first spring to life in the wake of a forest fire.

GALLBERRY (*Georgia*). Amber, flowing. Floral bouquet, pleasant, rich, flowery taste with a hint of caramel; slow to granulate. Nectar source: lowbush gallberry plants of the holly family, growing in the southern U.S. Good for baking as well as eating.

GOLDENROD (*United States*). Light amber with yellow tones, flowing. Distinctive aroma and flavor. All eighty species of the genus *Solidago* are native to North America, and the tasseled blossoms provide excellent nectar flow.

HAWAIIAN WHITE (*Hawaii*). White, softly crystallized. A very special, delicate honey made from the nectar of the tropical kiawe tree growing on the leeward side of the Big Island of Hawaii. Harvesting must be meticulously timed because this honey is quick to crystallize and can form solids in the comb if left too long. Uncompromising heat-free extraction by the beekeeper. Richard Spiegel, artisan producer. Connoisseur selection.

HEATHER (*Germany; Scotland; Ireland*). Dark amber, very thick. Rich, pungent flavor with hints of methanol and leather. Nectar source: *Calluna vulgaris*. Extremely high proportion of protein in heather honey gives it a unique, almost gelatinous, texture and contributes to its medicinal properties. Prized since ancient times. Connoisseur selection.

HOLLY (*Oregon*). Light amber, flowing. Rich flavor, slight tang with hints of apple and wintergreen. A winter source of nectar for the bees.

ITALIAN HONEYSUCKLE (*Italy*). White, naturally crystallized. Mild and sweet but multidimensional in flavor. Crystals are very small, producing a slightly chewy texture. Nectar source: a perennial raised as a fodder crop in the Mediterranean, not the flowering vine known as honeysuckle in the U.S. Artisan producer Giuseppe Coniglio of Sicily.

LAVENDER (*France; Spain*). Golden when liquid, white when creamed or granulated (granulates smoothly). Captures the perfume of the blossoms like no other honey; intense though mild, with slight astringency. Creamed French lavender honey is almost pure white and smoothly spreadable. Spanish lavender honey is also available. Connoisseur selection.

LEATHERWOOD (*Tasmania*). Light amber, softly "candied," as the Australians say. Spicy aroma, piquant flavor. It tastes like a flower. Distinctive among all the honeys of the world. Nectar source: white-flowered leatherwood trees in the southwestern rainforest of Tasmania. Unfiltered and unheated by the artisan producer Julian Wolfhagen; crystallization is carefully controlled to achieve the spreadable texture without using heat. Connoisseur selection.

LEHUA (*Hawaii*). Off-white, partly crystallized. Distinctive complex flavor. Tangy, not oversweet; crystallizes beautifully. Nectar source: the ohia tree, growing only in Hawaii. For many years, branches of lehua blossoms were offered to the volano Kilauea as an appeasement to the hot-tempered goddess Pele. Artisan producer in Hilo, and also Moon Shine Trading, a California packer of fine honeys.

 LEMON BLOSSOM (*Italy*). Very light gold, naturally crystallized. Not predominantly sweet. Clean light flavor with a zesty aftertaste. From artisan producer Giuseppe Coniglio of Sicily.

LIME (*Italy*). Light golden, naturally candied; said to be green-gold in color when liquid. Full-flavored with a zesty citrus element, particularly in the aftertaste, and a hint of wintergreen. Made from the pendant blossoms of the linden tree, in France, *tilleul* (a tilia, not a citrus; basswood is also a tilia).

MACADAMIA (*Hawaii*). Medium amber, flowing. Distinctive flavor, not sweet, complex, hints of roasted nuts and leather. Unique because macadamia trees grow only in Hawaii. Pollination by bees increases the nut set. Harvesting is tricky because the big bloom set on the trees occurs in November, when weather can be wet. Several days of sunshine are required for good nectar quality. Artisan producer in Papaikou. Silver spoon selection.

MANUKA (*New Zealand*). Amber, softly granulated. Unique moderately strong flavor, not sweet, complex medicinal blend of flavor including wintergreen. Nectar source: *Leptospermum scoparium* in remote native forests of New Zealand. Maori have gathered manuka honey for decades. It is antibacterial, antifungal, and credited with healing power. Its unusually high protein content creates viscosity and may contribute to its healing properties. Connoisseur selection.

MEADOWFOAM (*Oregon*). Light amber, flowing. Mild flavor with pronounced vanilla perfume.

MINT (*United States*). Amber, flowing. Flavor tends to mirror the flavor spectrum of thyme honey, only less intense; distinctive refreshing mint aftertaste. Nectar source: fields of mint already harvested (and allowed to bloom) for aromatic oils used to flavor many foods.

ORANGE BLOSSOM (*United States*). Light golden, flowing. Sweet, fruity flavor; sweet aftertaste with aroma of orange blossoms. Nectar source: may be made from a combination of citrus floral sources. Produced by bees used to pollinate large groves of orange growers in south Florida, Texas, Arizona, and California. Has been so widely available in the U.S. for decades, it is often thought of as "honey" flavor. Depending on the packer, can be merely sweet, or-in the case of the Laney Family Honey Company of Indiana—flushed with an orange color and a delight to taste, like orange candy.

PALMETTO (*Florida*). Light amber, flowing. Distinctive caramel flavor.

PINE (*Italy*). Dark amber, free flowing. Strong flavor, with menthol and leather tones. High mineral content is relevant for health applications. Honeydew source.

PUMPKIN BLOSSOM (*Oregon; California*). Medium amber, flowing. Rich flavor includes vanilla and hints of aged wood. Nectar sources: the pollination of seed crops. Less intense than chestnut honey but can be used in the same ways; complementary flavor for any squash recipe.

RASPBERRY (*Oregon; Washington*). Light amber, flowing; crystallizes readily. Mild, all-purpose honey, but especially good mixed with fresh berries. Nectar source: pollinators of raspberry crops. Here is the rare instance where a honey tastes like the fruit of the plant, although it is made from the flower's nectar. Berry flavor enhanced if eaten with plain yogurt.

REWAREWA (*New Zealand*). Golden with red tint. Texture of soft, sticky caramel. Mild, spicy, slightly burnt flavor; unusual. From the forests of North Island, New Zealand. Nectar source: a protea, *Knightia excelsa*, the New Zealand honeysuckle.

ROSEMARY (*Europe*). Light amber, partly crystallized. Herbal bouquet; not sweet, with a slight tang. Moderate intensity; nuance of smokiness. The legendary Narbonne honey of France was probably from rosemary. Artisan producer Pablo Laguna Rodriguez. Connoisseur selection.

SAGE (*western United States*). Light amber, flowing. The flavor is more floral than one might expect, at once rich and light. Nectar source: sage shrubs along the California coast and in the Sierra Nevadas. Widely available.

SNOWBERRY (*Oregon*). Light amber, flowing. Flavor delightfully suggests toasted marshmallow. Nectar source: *Symphoricarpos albus*, also found in Europe. On Mt. Hood, its winter-blooming habit provides a winter nectar source.

SOURWOOD (*North Carolina*). Amber, flowing, slow to crystallize. Distinctive mild, delicious flavor. This plant is one of those that does not produce pollen of use to bees.

STAR THISTLE (*California; Midwest; Oregon*). Light amber with a greenish-yellow tint, flowing. Flavor nicely nuanced with a slight tang. Although blossoms of star thistle are a bountiful honey source in various parts of the country, the plant is regarded as a pest by

California farmers because its extra-deep taproot makes it next to impossible to control. Excellent table honey.

SUNFLOWER (*United States; Spain*). Light amber with a yellow glow (my Spanish sample is a particularly flagrant yellow), flowing. Full-bodied flavor. Sunflower is such a prodigious nectar source (picture all the nectaries in a single, giant flower head) that it can be grown specifically for a honey.

THYME (*Italy; Greece*). Medium to dark amber, liquid or crystallized. One sort, from artisan producer Giuseppe Coniglio in Sicily, in a creamy crystallized state, is rich and full-flavored, not sweet, tangy, complex, with an herbal bouquet and a lingering taste resembling horehound. Thyme honey from other sources may include undertones of wintergreen and spice. Greek thyme honey is no longer the honey from Mt. Hymettus prized since ancient times, as the burgeoning population of Athens has virtually eliminated honey producers; but thyme honey from other parts of Greece can be special in their own way. High temperatures in the climate of many Greek locales create a particularly rich-flavored, dense honey. Connoisseur selection.

TUPELO (*Florida*). Light amber, lovely flowing texture (does not granulate). Floral bouquet, rich, mellow flavor. Made from nectar of tupelo trees in swamplands of northwestern Florida and southern Georgia. Hives may be placed on platforms on stilts high above the water and harvested by barge.

TULIP POPLAR (*United States*). Reddish amber, flowing. Not as strongly flavored as one would expect from a dark honey. It is tangy with hints of whiskey and a brown-sugar aftertaste. Widely available in the eastern United States. Nectar source: a tall, May-flowering tree, with large greenish-yellow blossoms found from southern New England to southern Michigan and south to the Gulf Coast states.

WILDFLOWER (*United States; Europe*). A name given to honey blended from different floral sources, also known as "multifloral" or "mixed floral" honey. Producers may choose to combine honeys from different known floral sources to create a flavorful, balanced blend. Bees also produce multifloral honey, especially later in the bloom season when they cannot rely on the nectar flow from a single source. Late-season blends tend to be darker in color than the earlier ones. Wildflower honey can be light amber to dark amber; flowing or creamed.

WILDFLOWER HONEY from Plan Bee in New York, bee-blended, is an intriguing combination of spice and perfume, especially in its creamed version, which is smooth but sticky with hints of butterscotch, clove, and mint.

SPRING WILDFLOWER from Ancient Nectars in Greece is amber, flowing. Taste includes a broad range of herbal tones, vaguely medicinal, with a slight smokiness.

THOUSAND FLOWERS HONEY from Catalonia is a highly perfumed blend of flavors.

DUNE COUNTRY HONEY from the Laney Family Honey Company in Indiana originates in the three counties that border on the south shore of Lake Michigan. Honey is light amber with distinctive flavor, sweet, light, and zesty.

WEST VIRGINIA WILDFLOWER from Thistledew Farms is dark amber in color, from bamboo along the Ohio River, not sweet, with a malty tang.

MISSOURI WILDFLOWER. medium amber, is rich and mellow, with the refinement of a Cuban cigar.

FOXGLOVE AND WILDFLOWER from Oregon is light in color, tastes of vanilla and malt.

Recipes

Choosing the honey to use in a recipe is often an uncomplicated matter; you just use honey you have on hand, and the result will taste good. The specific honey is usually not the most important aspect of a dish. Generally, a mild honey is a good choice when no pronounced honey flavor is wanted. Clover, alfalfa, and other mild blends work well in any recipe in this collection. Dark honey is particularly delicious in spiced cakes and cookies. Sometimes a recipe specifies a certain honey that I found particularly effective. Some of the recipes call for honey only, and some require both honey (for flavor) and sugar (for texture).

A honey with a powerful flavor of its own, like an aromatic orange blossom, can assert its flavor over all the other ingredients, so you would not select it when you want a blended taste. Some dishes take on a different character according to the honey you use, from mild to dark, and only you will know which one suits your palate best. Certain dishes provide a great opportunity for experimenting with the flavor effect of different choices, like Honey-Vanilla Custard (page 116), Honey Ice Cream (page 123), or Walnut Honey Bread (page 37).

Cakes or breads that are made with honey tend to brown more readily and stay fresh longer than those made with sugar. Both facts may be attributed to the fructose content of honey. Fructose browns more intensely at oven temperatures than glucose or sucrose and is very hygroscopic, absorbing moisture from the air and preventing staling. Commercial baked goods often include honey so that they will look better and have longer life.

Chefs of the nineties have learned to use honey as a condiment, much as they have learned to use just a splash of very special vinegar or olive oil, judiciously applied. Chestnut honey, curiously unsweet in nature, is a particular darling of menus in the best restaurants around the San Francisco Bay Area. This Italian honey combines well with simple white cheeses like Greek *manouri*—a chunk of cheese drizzled with chestnut honey, plated with a few toasted walnuts, makes a fashionable end to a meal. The same combination on a water biscuit makes a great appetizer to pass around. Strong dark honey is featured in this part of the world with strong blue cheese and may appear on salad plates or for dessert. Or honey is respectfully used as a flavoring agent—as in Lindsey Shere's lavender-scented honey ice cream served at Chez Panisse in Berkeley. Chefs these days love to roast fruits as well as vegetables, and nothing could be more delicious with roasted figs than the burnish of a little honey.

All over the world, honey is probably most frequently used as a spread for good, fresh bread; for the French *tartine*, a buttered baguette ready to receive honey or jam; as a topping for Italian *pane* or Mexican *bolillos*. Among the recipes here are formulas for breads that underscore the flavor of honey—nutty whole-grain loaves; muffins, pancakes, flaky biscuits, flamboyant squash cornbread—that are perfect brought hot to the table ready for honey and butter. The even simpler method of eating honey from a spoon is unsurpassed as a way to appreciate the pure flavor of honey.

Honey baking has also figured in traditional pastries in Europe and Asia for centuries, partly because of the keeping quality honey lends to baked goods. Gingerbread and other versions of spiced honey loaves probably spring from a simple honey-and-flour bread created by the Chinese in the tenth century. Genghis Khan's Mongol horsemen in the thirteenth century are said to have carried a nourishing flour-and-honey cake in their saddlebags and to have passed on the taste for it to the Turks and Arabs. Only after the thirteenth century did sucrose sweeteners become available and eventually supplant honey because of their relatively cheap price. We retain a treasure trove of cakes, breads, honey-soaked pastries, and cookies that bear the stamp of different cultures in taking advantage of the special virtues of honey.

BREADS
and
MUFFINS

The Cheese Board's Egg and Honey Bread

Delicious fresh breads are made daily at the Cheese Board, a busy shop in Berkeley crammed with an astonishing variety of the finest quality cheeses. They bake foccacia and scones as well as baguettes and solid country loaves. This bread makes a fantastic toasted cheese sandwich, with the tang of sharp cheddar cheese set off by the slightly sweet bread.

YIELD: 4 LOAVES

1 TABLESPOON ACTIVE DRY YEAST
1 TEASPOON SUGAR
1 CUP WARM WATER
1 CUP WHOLE MILK
4 TABLESPOONS HONEY
1 TABLESPOON SALT
2 EGGS
3 TABLESPOONS UNSALTED BUTTER
6 TO 8 CUPS UNBLEACHED WHITE FLOUR

Dissolve the yeast and sugar in the warm water in a medium ceramic bowl and set in a warm, draft-free place until it bubbles vigorously. Heat the milk to boiling in a small saucepan. Place the honey, salt, eggs, and butter in a large mixing bowl or the bowl of a heavy-duty mixer, and pour the hot milk over them. Stir to combine and cool to lukewarm.

Add 1 cup of the flour and then add the yeast mixture. Add flour a few cups at a time, mixing thoroughly, until you have a smooth dough that clears the sides of the bowl. Turn out onto a lightly floured surface and knead until shiny and elastic.

Form into a ball and place in a greased bowl, cover, and set in a warm place to rise until double. Punch it down with a single blow of your fist and divide into four parts.

Shape into neat, firm balls of dough that are well sealed, and place them in four small, greased foil pie pans. Place these on a baking sheet, well separated, for ease in handling. Allow dough to rise again, covered, until double.

Preheat the oven to 350°. Bake the loaves 30 to 40 minutes, until rich golden brown and hollow sounding when thumped. Remove them from the pans and transfer to racks to cool.

MILK AND HONEY LOAF

Eat this wholesome bread cooled, with lots of butter. Keeps a day or two, well wrapped.

YIELD: 1 LOAF

1 CUP GRAHAM FLOUR
1 CUP UNBLEACHED WHITE FLOUR
2 TEASPOONS BAKING POWDER
½ TEASPOON SALT
1 CUP WHOLE MILK
½ CUP DARK HONEY, SUCH AS BUCKWHEAT

Butter a 7 by 3-inch loaf pan. Preheat the oven to 375°. Put the graham flour in a mixing bowl. Sift the white flour, baking powder, and salt over the graham flour. Measure the milk in a 2-cup measure and incorporate the honey at a drizzle. Pour the milk and honey mixture into the flour and beat until well combined. Pour into the loaf pan and bake 40 to 50 minutes, until humped and well browned.

Hearty Graham Bread

Firm and delicious, this is my favorite all-purpose bread. Simply wonderful with butter and honey.

YIELD: 4 LOAVES

1/4 CUP UNSALTED BUTTER

3 TABLESPOONS GOLDEN HONEY, SUCH AS ALFALFA

1 TABLESPOON SALT

1 LARGE CAN (12 OUNCES) EVAPORATED MILK

1 ADDITIONAL CAN (1 1/2 CUPS) HOT WATER

1 TABLESPOON ACTIVE DRY YEAST

1 TEASPOON SUGAR OR HONEY

1/4 TEASPOON GROUND DRIED GINGER

1/2 CUP WARM WATER

5 CUPS UNBLEACHED WHITE FLOUR PLUS ADDITIONAL AS NEEDED

3 CUPS GRAHAM FLOUR

Place the butter, honey, salt, and evaporated milk in a large bowl or the bowl of a heavy-duty mixer. Pour the hot water over, mix, and cool to lukewarm. Shortly before it is cooled, place the yeast, sugar, ginger, and warm water in a small ceramic bowl and set in a warm, draft-free place until it bubbles vigorously.

Mix 1 cup of the white flour in the cooled milk mixture. Add the yeast mixture, then the graham flour, and additional white flour as needed to make an elastic and shiny dough that readily leaves the sides of the bowl. Turn out onto a floured board and knead until uniformly smooth and elastic. Place in a large, greased ceramic bowl, cover, and set in a warm place to double in bulk. Grease four 8 by 4-inch loaf pans.

When the dough has doubled, punch it down with a single blow of your fist. Work the dough together again and divide it into four parts. Roll each portion with a rolling pin into a rectangle about 8 by 12 inches and roll it up very tightly, as for a jellyroll, from the narrower side.

Pinch the long seam securely, turn this to the bottom, and tuck the ends under smoothly, pinching into place. Place in the prepared pans and let rise until half again as large.

Preheat the oven to 375°. Bake about 1 hour, until well browned and hollow sounding when thumped. Remove from pans at once and transfer to racks to cool.

RICOTTA PANCAKES

Ricotta cheese deserves to be more widely used; its taste is fresh and simple, like well-made cottage cheese. Serve these pancakes with honey, jam, or fresh fruit.

YIELD: 4 SERVINGS

1 CUP RICOTTA CHEESE
3 EGGS
2 TABLESPOONS BLAND OIL
⅓ CUP UNBLEACHED WHITE FLOUR
2 TEASPOONS MILD HONEY
¼ TEASPOON SALT

Combine the cheese, eggs, oil, flour, honey, and salt in a blender jar and blend until smooth, about 5 minutes, scraping the sides of the jar as needed. (Another method is to sieve the cheese into a bowl and beat in the remaining ingredients until smooth.) Fry in 3-inch cakes on a well-buttered heavy frying pan or griddle over medium heat, turning the cakes when bubbles appear. Serve at once.

ENGLISH MUFFINS WITH CURRANTS

These muffins include whole-wheat flour and currants for extra taste and nutrition, but you can easily make the plain style. Good form requires that you split English muffins with a fork, creating the maximum number of craters for butter to melt into. Toast and serve with lots of butter and honey.

YIELD: ABOUT 10 MUFFINS

1 CUP WHOLE MILK
2 TABLESPOONS MILD HONEY, SUCH AS CLOVER
1 TEASPOON SALT
3 TABLESPOONS UNSALTED BUTTER
½ CUP CURRANTS
1 TABLESPOON ACTIVE DRY YEAST
1 CUP WARM WATER
1 TEASPOON SUGAR OR HONEY
1½ CUPS WHOLE-WHEAT FLOUR
4 CUPS UNBLEACHED WHITE FLOUR
CORNMEAL, FOR SHAPING

Scald the milk in a small heavy saucepan. Stir in the honey, salt, butter, and currants and cool to lukewarm. In a small ceramic bowl, combine the yeast, water, and sugar and set in a warm, draft-free place until it bubbles vigorously. Place the whole-wheat flour and 1½ cups of the white flour in a large bowl or the bowl of a heavy-duty mixer. Add the yeast mixture and combine thoroughly. Add the milk mixture and beat until smooth. Stir in the remaining 2½ cups of flour to make a stiff dough. Turn out onto a floured board and knead briefly until it forms a manageable ball. (Some stickiness is all right.) Place the ball in a greased bowl, turning it once to grease the top. Cover and let rise in a warm place until doubled, about 1 hour.

Punch down the dough and divide it in half. Grease a baking sheet and cover a pastry board with a thick layer of cornmeal and place the dough on it. Pat each half of the dough into a

½-inch-thick rectangle. Cut circles in the dough using a floured 3- or 4-inch cutter. Place the muffins 2 inches apart on the baking sheet, cover, and let rise until doubled, about 45 minutes. Heat a heavy frying pan or griddle and butter lightly. Place the muffins on it, cornmeal side down first, and bake 10 minutes on each side, until well browned. Transfer to wire racks to cool.

WALNUT HONEY BREAD

YIELD: 1 LOAF

1 CUP WHOLE MILK
1 CUP HONEY, MILD OR DARK
¼ CUP SUGAR
¼ CUP UNSALTED BUTTER
2 EGG YOLKS
1½ CUPS UNBLEACHED WHITE FLOUR
1 TEASPOON SALT
1 TEASPOON BAKING SODA
½ CUP WALNUTS, BROKEN

Butter and flour a 9 by 5-inch loaf pan. In a large saucepan, heat the milk. Add the honey and sugar, stirring until the sugar is melted and homogeneous. Cool. Mix in the butter and egg yolks. Sift together the flour, salt, and baking soda. Add the dry ingredients to the honey mixture and mix in thoroughly. Stir in the walnuts. Pour into the pan and let stand 20 minutes. Preheat the oven to 325°. Bake about 1 hour, until a toothpick inserted in the center comes out clean. Cool in the pan 10 minutes, then remove and transfer to a rack to cool. Wrap well and store. It tastes better the second day.

BASIC RICH COFFEECAKE DOUGH

Supple and easily shaped, this basic dough lends itself to a variety of fillings, and the large quantity can be used to make a number of different breads, like the Honey Almond Twist (page 39) and Sticky Buns (page 42). Baking the plain dough in loaves or buns gives a brioche-like bread, moist and good for toasting.

YIELD: FOUR 9 BY 5-INCH LOAVES OR EQUIVALENT SHAPES

1 CUP UNSALTED BUTTER
¾ CUP PLUS 4 TEASPOONS SUGAR
2 TEASPOONS SALT
1½ CUPS HOT WHOLE MILK
4 TABLESPOONS ACTIVE DRY YEAST
1 TEASPOON GROUND DRIED GINGER
1 CUP WARM WATER
6 WHOLE EGGS
6 EGG YOLKS
GRATED RIND OF 1 LEMON
8 TO 10 CUPS UNBLEACHED WHITE FLOUR

Place the butter, ¼ cup sugar, and salt in a large mixing bowl or the bowl of a heavy-duty mixer. Pour the hot milk over it, stir once or twice, and let cool to lukewarm. Meanwhile mix together the yeast, 4 teaspoons sugar, ginger, and warm water in a small ceramic bowl and place in a warm draft-free place until it bubbles vigorously. To the milk mixture, add the eggs and egg yolks and beat well. Grate the lemon directly into the bowl so that no aromatic oils are lost. Add 1 cup of the flour, mix well, and add the yeast mixture. Continue adding flour until you have a smooth, medium-soft dough that is shiny and elastic. Knead until it cleans the sides of the bowl.

Cover with a towel and set in a warm place to rise, about 1½ hours. Divide into desired portions. If you are making plain loaves, divide into four parts and shape into loaves. Let rise again until doubled, 30 to 45 minutes. Preheat oven to 350°. Bake for 45 minutes to 1 hour, until browned and firm.

Honey Almond Twist

At my grandfather's German bakery in Chicago in the early 1900s they made a coffeecake like this one with the name Bienenstich, which means "beesting." I have never been sure if this was a joke or if it was one of those odd slips in language. Bienenstock would mean "beehive," and the twisted coil of dough used to create the coffeecake does have a certain likeness to a traditional skep-shaped hive.

YIELD: 1 LOAF

1 LOAF BASIC RICH COFFEECAKE DOUGH (PAGE 38)
¼ CUP MILD HONEY
¼ CUP SUGAR
¼ CUP UNSALTED BUTTER
¼ CUP UNBLEACHED WHITE FLOUR
½ CUP SLICED UNBLANCHED ALMONDS

Prepare the dough. Butter a 10-inch round baking pan (a springform pan or a skillet). Shape the dough into a long rope less than 1 inch in diameter by rolling it between your hands and a bread board. Place the dough rope in the pan, starting at the outer edge and twisting continuously as you coil toward the center. Cover the pan loosely with a damp towel, set in a warm place, and let rise until double. When the dough has risen so that the pan surface is completely filled in, preheat the oven to 375°. Mix the honey, sugar, butter, flour, and almonds together. Spread the topping gently over the dough, avoiding the outer edge (which burns too quickly). Bake about 30 minutes, until golden. Leave in pan 5 minutes, then remove and transfer to a rack to cool.

ETHIOPIAN HONEY-SPICE BREAD

Coriander is perhaps the oldest spice known to man. The seeds of coriander have been found in Egyptian tombs, and Old Testament references to this spice show that it was well known to early Jews. Originally native to the Mediterranean area, coriander now grows throughout the world. Although coriander was the favored spice of American colonial cookie bakers, few modern Americans can identify the flavor. This Ethiopian honey bread, with its lively flavor and fragrance, is a strong argument for keeping a jar of ground coriander on the shelf. While this bread is delicious plain, it is traditionally spread with butter and honey. It keeps exceedingly well.

YIELD: 1 LOAF

1 TABLESPOON ACTIVE DRY YEAST
¼ CUP WARM WATER
1 TEASPOON SUGAR OR HONEY
⅛ TEASPOON GROUND DRIED GINGER
1 EGG
½ CUP MILD HONEY
1 TABLESPOON GROUND CORIANDER
½ TEASPOON GROUND CINNAMON
¼ TEASPOON GROUND CLOVES
1½ TEASPOONS SALT
1 CUP WHOLE MILK, WARMED
4 TABLESPOONS UNSALTED BUTTER, MELTED AND COOLED
4½ CUPS UNBLEACHED WHITE FLOUR

Combine the yeast, water, sugar, and ginger in a small ceramic bowl and set in a warm, draft-free place until it bubbles vigorously. Combine the egg, honey, spices, and salt in a large mixing bowl or the bowl of a heavy-duty mixer. Add the milk and the butter. Mix in 1 cup of the flour.

Add the yeast mixture and beat until all the ingredients are well blended. Add more flour ½ cup at a time, using only enough to make a soft dough. Use your hands, if needed, to work in the last flour. Turn out onto a lightly floured surface and knead the bread by folding it end to end, pressing down and pushing forward several times with the heel of your hand. (The dough will be sticky. Use a dough scraper to clear the board and turn the mass of dough. Avoid adding more flour.)

In about 5 minutes the dough will become smoother and more elastic. Shape into a rough ball and place in a large bowl, covered, to rise until double in bulk.

Butter heavily a 3-quart round baking dish that is 3 inches deep, such as a casserole or enameled Dutch oven. Punch down the dough with a single blow of your fist. Knead the dough for a few minutes, shape into a rough ball, and place in the prepared pan. (Press the dough down so that the bottom of the pan is covered completely.) Cover and let rise again until doubled, reaching the top of the pan.

Preheat the oven to 300°. Bake 50 to 60 minutes, until nicely rounded on top and a light golden brown. Leave in pan 5 minutes, then remove and transfer to a rack to cool.

STICKY BUNS

The combination of butter and honey is wonderful as the basis for sticky buns. The glaze is very glossy and delicious. A heavy-weight non-stick pan works particularly well here.

YIELD: 9 BUNS

1 LOAF BASIC RICH COFFEECAKE DOUGH (PAGE 38)
2 TABLESPOONS UNSALTED BUTTER, MELTED
$\frac{1}{2}$ TEASPOON GROUND CINNAMON
$\frac{1}{2}$ CUP CHOPPED PRUNES
$\frac{1}{4}$ CUP CANDIED LEMON PEEL (PAGE 54)
2 TABLESPOONS PLUS $\frac{1}{2}$ CUP GOLDEN HONEY, SUCH AS ALFALFA OR SUNFLOWER
$\frac{1}{4}$ CUP CHOPPED BLANCHED ALMONDS

Roll the dough into a rectangle about 9 by 12 inches. Spread with the melted butter and sprinkle with the cinnamon. Combine the prunes, lemon peel, 2 tablespoons honey, and nuts and spread evenly over the dough. Butter a 9-inch square baking pan lavishly and put $\frac{1}{2}$ cup of honey in the bottom of the pan. Roll up the dough tightly, starting with the short side. Cut into nine pieces about 1 inch thick, and place them cut side down in the pan. Place pan in a warm location, cover with a damp towel, and allow to rise until doubled, 30 to 40 minutes.

Preheat the oven to 375°. Bake 30 minutes, until well browned and firm. Let cool in the pan a few minutes, then turn out onto a plate to cool.

Variation: May also be baked in a muffin tin. Prepare the tin by buttering each section and adding 2 teaspoons of honey. Prepare the dough as above and cut into twelve pieces about 1-inch thick. Place each, cut side down, in a muffin section. Set the pan in a warm location, cover with a damp towel, and let rise until the dough is above the edge of the pan. Bake as directed.

AUNT VAN'S OATMEAL BREAD

Serve for breakfast with butter and honey, or with soup for lunch.

YIELD: 2 LOAVES

1⅓ CUPS BOILING WATER
1 CUP ROLLED OATS
3 TEASPOONS SALT
1 TABLESPOON UNSALTED BUTTER
½ CUP DARK HONEY, SUCH AS BUCKWHEAT
2 TABLESPOONS ACTIVE DRY YEAST
½ CUP WARM WATER
1 TEASPOON SUGAR OR HONEY
¼ TEASPOON GROUND DRIED GINGER
5½ CUPS UNBLEACHED WHITE FLOUR

Pour the boiling water over the oats in a bowl. Add the salt, butter, and honey, and let the mixture sit for 1 hour. Shortly before the hour is up, combine the yeast, warm water, sugar, and ginger in a small bowl and set in a warm, draft-free place until it bubbles actively. Combine the yeast with 5 cups of the flour. Then add the oatmeal mixture and stir well to make a stiff dough. Turn out onto a board covered with the remaining ½ cup flour and knead well, until the dough is smooth, shiny, and elastic.

Form into a ball and place in a greased bowl, turning once to grease the top. Cover and let rise in a warm place until doubled, about 1 hour.

Butter two 8 by 4-inch loaf pans. Punch down the dough with a single blow of the fist. Knead briefly. Divide in half and form into loaves. Place in the pans and let rise until double. Preheat oven to 375° and bake for 40 minutes, until nicely browned and hollow sounding when thumped. Transfer to racks to cool.

Dark Banana Bread

Banana bread became an American staple because of its good flavor and adaptability—sandwiched with cream cheese it makes a meal, and it keeps so well it is ready for a snack or dessert whenever needed. This version includes wheat germ and whole-wheat flour for extra goodness.

YIELD: 1 LOAF

1 CUP UNBLEACHED WHITE FLOUR
1 CUP WHOLE-WHEAT FLOUR
¼ CUP RAW WHEAT GERM
½ TEASPOON SALT
1 TEASPOON BAKING SODA
½ CUP UNSALTED BUTTER
¾ CUP GOLDEN HONEY
2 EGGS, BEATEN
1 CUP MASHED, VERY RIPE BANANAS (ABOUT 3)
2 TO 3 TABLESPOONS HOT WATER
½ CUP CHOPPED NUTS, DATES, OR RAISINS

Preheat the oven to 325°. Butter a 9 by 5-inch loaf pan. Combine the white flour, whole-wheat flour, wheat germ, salt, and soda in a medium bowl and set aside.

In a large, heavy saucepan, melt the butter and stir in the honey until evenly mixed and just lukewarm. Add the eggs and banana, combining thoroughly. Stir in the dry ingredients in two parts, adding the hot water between additions to make a light, smooth dough. Stir in nuts or fruits as desired. Push into the prepared pan, level the surface, and bake 70 minutes, or until humped, brown, and firm to the touch. Cool in the pan on a rack. Turn out, wrap well, and store a day before slicing.

FLAKY BISCUITS

Honey and biscuits are a perfect pair, each bringing out the best in the other. This recipe makes biscuits that puff into flaky layers. For soft Southern-style tear-apart biscuits, you can't do better than to follow the recipe on the package of self-rising flour ordered direct from The White Lily Food Company in Knoxville, Tennessee (phone 800-264-5459). Whatever biscuits you bake, follow the rule of impeccable freshness and serve hot with honey and real butter. Honeycomb will melt into hot biscuits—try it if you don't believe me.

YIELD: 12 BISCUITS

2 CUPS UNBLEACHED WHITE FLOUR
3 TEASPOONS BAKING POWDER
¾ TEASPOON SALT
½ CUP PLUS 2 TABLESPOONS UNSALTED BUTTER, COLD
½ CUP WHOLE MILK, COLD
2 EGGS, WELL BEATEN

Sift the flour, baking powder, and salt into a mixing bowl. With a pastry blender, cut in the ½ cup butter until the mixture has the texture of meal. Put the milk in a large measuring cup, drop in the eggs, and beat together. Pour this into the flour mixture and combine lightly with a fork. (It is better to have a few loose flour particles than to overmix.) On a floured board, roll this dough into a ½-inch-thick rectangle. Preheat the oven to 475°.

Over the lowest two-thirds of the dough, distribute the 2 tablespoons of butter cut into small pieces. Work quickly so that the butter does not warm up. Fold the upper third over the middle of the dough and the lower third over that. Turn this rectangle halfway around on the board, roll again to ½-inch-thick, and fold and roll again. Cut the ½-inch-thick dough into squares 1½ inches across and place them, slightly separated, on an ungreased baking sheet. Bake about 10 minutes, until puffed and brown.

Variation: Make larger biscuits, split, and serve with crushed berries as shortcake.

Squash Cornbread

Bright color and extra moistness result from using squash in this recipe. I suspect that pumpkin and sweet potatoes would do very nicely, too. Serve hot with lots of butter. Also excellent toasted the next day, with butter and honey.

YIELD: 6 TO 8 SLICES OR ONE 9-INCH BREAD

1 TEASPOON BAKING SODA

1 CUP BUTTERMILK

1 CUP SOUR CREAM

2 TABLESPOONS MILD HONEY

2 EGGS

$^3/_4$ CUP MASHED COOKED SQUASH, AT ROOM TEMPERATURE

2 CUPS CORNMEAL

1$^1/_2$ TEASPOONS SALT

1$^1/_2$ TABLESPOONS UNSALTED BUTTER

Preheat the oven to 350°. Dissolve the soda in the buttermilk. Stir in the sour cream and incorporate the honey in a thin stream. In a medium mixing bowl, beat the eggs and add the squash, cornmeal, salt, and buttermilk mixture. In a 9-inch pie plate or baking dish, melt the butter. Tilt the pan to coat the dish well, then pour the excess into the batter (1 tablespoon), stirring to incorporate. Pour the batter into the baking dish. Bake 30 to 40 minutes, until set at the center.

Opposite page, from top to bottom: Sticky Buns (page 42), Squash Cornbread (above), Ethiopian Honey Spice Bread (page 40), and Honey Butter (page 127).

California Orange Muffins

Nutty with wheat germ and fragrant with orange, these muffins are irresistible at any meal. Serve with butter and honey.

YIELD: 12 MUFFINS

1 CUP SIFTED UNBLEACHED WHITE FLOUR
1 TEASPOON BAKING POWDER
1/4 TEASPOON BAKING SODA
1/2 TEASPOON SALT
1/2 CUP RAW WHEAT GERM
1/4 CUP UNSALTED BUTTER, AT ROOM TEMPERATURE
1/4 CUP ORANGE BLOSSOM HONEY
1 EGG, BEATEN
GRATED RIND OF 1 ORANGE
1/2 CUP FRESHLY SQUEEZED ORANGE JUICE

Preheat the oven to 375°. Butter a muffin tin. Sift the flour with the baking powder, soda, and salt. Add the wheat germ and set aside. Cream the butter, add the honey, and beat until smooth and fluffy. Blend in the egg, orange rind, and orange juice. Add the dry ingredients to the creamed mixture, stirring just until all the ingredients are moist. (The batter will look lumpy.) Fill the greased tins two-thirds full and bake for 20 minutes, until muffins are rounded and brown. Turn out immediately, bundle in a cloth-lined basket, and bring to the table.

Buttermilk Bran Muffins

Simply the best bran muffins ever.

YIELD: 12 MUFFINS

1 CUP UNBLEACHED WHITE FLOUR
3 CUPS WHOLE BRAN
1 TEASPOON BAKING POWDER
½ TEASPOON BAKING SODA
1 TEASPOON SALT
⅓ CUP UNSALTED BUTTER, AT ROOM TEMPERATURE
¼ CUP FIRMLY PACKED BROWN SUGAR
¼ CUP GOLDEN HONEY, SUCH AS ALFALFA, PLUS MORE FOR TOPPING
1 EGG
⅞ CUP BUTTERMILK (1 CUP MINUS 2 TABLESPOONS)

Preheat the oven to 400°. Grease a muffin tin with oil. Blend the flour, bran, baking powder, soda, and salt and set aside. (This may be done the night before to minimize preparation time in the morning if they are to be breakfast muffins.) Cream the butter, sugar, honey, and egg. Stir in the dry ingredients alternately with the buttermilk, just until all ingredients are moistened. Avoid beating. Fill the prepared pan two-thirds full and drizzle about 1 teaspoon of honey over the top of each muffin. Bake 20 to 25 minutes. Turn out of pans immediately and serve hot with butter.

Fresh Blueberry Muffins

A basic muffin to be varied according to the fruit of the season. Serve muffins fresh from the oven topped with honey and butter.

YIELD: 12 MUFFINS

1 CUP WHOLE-WHEAT FLOUR
1½ TEASPOONS BAKING POWDER
½ TEASPOON SALT
½ CUP FRESH BLUEBERRIES, WASHED AND DRIED
½ CUP SOUR CREAM
1 TABLESPOON HONEY
1 EGG
2 TO 4 TABLESPOONS BUTTERMILK, AS NEEDED

Preheat the oven to 375°. Grease a muffin tin with oil. Sift together into a medium mixing bowl the flour, baking powder, and salt. Toss the berries lightly through this mixture. (This helps keep them from sinking to the bottom.) In a large measuring cup, measure the sour cream and add the honey and egg, mixing it all together. Add to the dry ingredients, combining lightly. Add enough buttermilk to make a soft dough. Spoon into the prepared tin and bake 20 to 25 minutes, until golden and firm to a gentle touch.

Variation: *Substitute drained canned cherries, frozen raspberries, or chopped sweetened cranberries for the blueberries, or use a smaller amount of dried berries.*

ORANGE-PECAN WAFFLES

Serve these waffles with Honey Butter (page 127) or other toppings as desired.

YIELD: 6 TO 8 WAFFLES

2 CUPS SIFTED CAKE FLOUR
1 TABLESPOON BAKING POWDER
1 TEASPOON SALT
3 EGGS, SEPARATED
2 TABLESPOONS MILD HONEY
1 CUP WHOLE MILK
½ CUP BLAND OIL
¼ CUP FRESHLY SQUEEZED ORANGE JUICE
GRATED RIND OF 1 LARGE ORANGE
PECANS, ALMONDS, OR WALNUTS, CHOPPED

Preheat a waffle iron. Sift together the flour, baking powder, and salt and set aside. Beat the egg yolks with a wire whisk, then add the honey, milk, oil, orange juice, and orange rind. Blend well. Stir in the dry ingredients, mixing until smooth.

Beat the egg whites until stiff but not dry. Stir one-fourth of the whites into the batter to lighten it. Gently but thoroughly fold in the rest, using a rubber spatula. Ladle out onto the hot waffle iron, sprinkle with nuts to taste, and bake. (The waffles are done when the steam stops appearing at the sides.) The waffles should be golden and crisp.

Orange Doughnuts with Honey Syrup

An unusual breakfast treat, easy to prepare if one has an extra half hour one morning and a jar of basic honey syrup on hand. The doughnuts are best eaten at once. Provide plenty of napkins for your guests, since they are sticky.

YIELD: 12 SMALL DOUGHNUTS

1 CUP BASIC HONEY SYRUP FOR PASTRIES (PAGE 126)
2 EGGS
¼ CUP BLAND OIL
¼ CUP SUGAR
¼ CUP FRESHLY SQUEEZED ORANGE JUICE
GRATED RIND OF 1 ORANGE
2 CUPS UNBLEACHED WHITE FLOUR
1 TABLESPOON BAKING SODA
OIL FOR DEEP FRYING

Prepare the honey syrup and set aside. Combine the eggs, oil, sugar, orange juice, and orange rind in a medium bowl, stirring until smooth. Sift the flour with the baking soda and add to the egg mixture, beating constantly until the mixture is thick and falls from the spoon in a ribbon. Cover and set aside for about 30 minutes.

Heat the oil in a deep saucepan to 350°. (The oil should be deep but not fill the pan, lest it bubble over the sides when the doughnuts are added.) While the oil is heating, warm up the honey syrup. To shape the doughnuts, flour your hands heavily and gather the dough into a ball. Divide into twelve equal parts. In your hands, roll each part into a ball, flatten it in your palm, and poke a hole through the middle with a finger. Keep your hands well floured to prevent sticking. Fry the doughnuts without crowding for 3 to 5 minutes, turning once, until golden brown. Drain on paper towels. When all the doughnuts are cooked and drained, prick them in two or three places with a fork, pick them up with tongs and dip them into the honey syrup. Eat at once.

FRUITS
and
VEGETABLES

CANDIED LEMON AND ORANGE PEELS

YIELD: APPROXIMATELY 2 CUPS

4 ORANGES
2 LEMONS
2 CUPS WATER
2 CUPS SUGAR

Remove the peel from oranges and lemons in wide wedges, including the white pith but none of the fruit pulp. Blanch the peel in a large kettle of boiling water for 5 minutes. Drain and repeat with fresh water up to five times. Drain and cool. Trim the soft rind into uniform ¼-inch strips.

Prepare a simple syrup in a large, heavy saucepan with the water and sugar. Stir over medium heat until the sugar is dissolved, then simmer about 10 minutes until it thickens.

Drop the rind into the hot syrup and cook, partially covered, until the rind is translucent and impregnated with syrup, about 40 minutes. Cool the rind in the syrup.

Cover a 10 by 15-inch baking pan with a light coating of granulated sugar. When the peel is cool, lift from the syrup, draining off any excess, and place in a single layer in the pan. Let dry uncovered overnight. Then place in an airtight container for storage. Peel stored this way keeps for a few weeks. Freeze for longer storage.

NOTE: I blanch oranges and lemons together, although purists may wish to follow the one fruit–one pot rule. I save any leftover syrup in the refrigerator and add sugar and water in equal parts to make the volume needed for another batch. Pineapple, cut into large wedges or bite-sized pieces, may also be candied this way. Do not combine pineapple with other fruit in blanching or finishing. To make fruit peel confections with longer shelf life, scrape the white pulp from the peel after blanching and proceed as directed.

GREEN GRAPES WITH PORT

YIELD: 6 SERVINGS

1 POUND SEEDLESS GREEN GRAPES
1 TEASPOON FRESHLY SQUEEZED LEMON JUICE
2 TABLESPOONS PORT
1/4 CUP MILD HONEY

Wash and stem the grapes. Stir the lemon juice, port, and honey together in a non-metal bowl that can be covered easily. Mix in the grapes, cover, and refrigerate for 4 hours or more. Serve in dessert dishes, spooning the juices over the grapes.

SPICY HONEYED CARROTS

YIELD: 4 SERVINGS

1/4 CUP UNSALTED BUTTER
6 CARROTS, PEELED AND CUT INTO JULIENNE STRIPS
1/4 TEASPOON SALT
2 TEASPOONS MILD HONEY
1/2 TEASPOON DRY MUSTARD
FRESHLY GROUND PEPPER

In a large frying pan with a cover, melt the butter. Add the carrots, sprinkle with the salt, and cover tightly. Steam the carrots over medium heat in the butter until tender, 15 to 30 minutes. Combine the honey, mustard, and pepper to taste, and add to the pan, stirring and turning frequently to coat the carrots evenly. Simmer a few minutes and serve at once.

GRAND MARNIER SUMMER COMPOTE

YIELD: 6 SERVINGS

4 LARGE PEACHES, PEELED
1 TEASPOON FRESHLY SQUEEZED LEMON JUICE
1/2 CUP FRESH BLUEBERRIES
3 TABLESPOONS FRESHLY SQUEEZED ORANGE JUICE
1 TABLESPOON GRAND MARNIER OR CURAÇAO
1 1/2 TABLESPOONS HONEY

Cut the peaches into thick slices and place in a serving bowl. Sprinkle with the lemon juice to prevent discoloration. Add the blueberries. Combine the orange juice, liqueur, and honey and pour over the fruit, mixing gently. Cover and marinate in the refrigerator for at least 1 hour. Other fruits may be used depending on the season.

REFRESHING FRUIT SMOOTHIE

You can use any combination of fruit that appeals to you to make this refreshing snack. If you are not using frozen fruit, add a couple of ice cubes to the mix.

YIELD: 2 CUPS, 1 GENEROUS SERVING

2 TABLESPOONS GOLDEN HONEY, OR MORE TO TASTE
1/2 CUP FRESHLY SQUEEZED ORANGE JUICE
1/2 CUP SLICED BANANA
1/2 CUP PLAIN LOWFAT YOGURT
3/4 CUP FROZEN MIXED FRUITS (STRAWBERRIES, RASPBERRIES, BLUEBERRIES),
    STRAIGHT FROM FREEZER

Place all ingredients in the jar of a blender and whirl until smooth. Pour into a tall glass to serve.

Plum Salad

Highly seasonal, this salad is a delicious celebration of the days of high summer when there are plums of many colors in the markets. Choose several distinctly different kinds—sweet yellow, firm dark red, or prune plums with yellow, slightly mealy, interiors.

YIELD: SERVINGS DEPEND ON AMOUNT OF FRUIT USED

RIPE FRESH PLUMS, FOUR VARIETIES IF POSSIBLE
SOUR CREAM
HONEY

Cut the plums into quarters with as little violence as possible around the pits. Arrange in a serving dish and dollop sour cream generously around the bowl. Drizzle honey liberally over the arrangement.

Honeydew Ginger

A refreshing dessert or brunch dish.

YIELD:6 SERVINGS

1 TABLESPOON HONEY
1 TEASPOON GROUND DRIED GINGER
6 WEDGES RIPE HONEYDEW MELON

Mix together the honey and ground ginger in a small bowl. Drizzle over the wedges of honey-dew melon.

Carrots in Pomegranate Sauce

From early times, people of the arid Middle East have esteemed the pomegranate for its refreshing juice. King Solomon had an orchard of pomegranates. Mohammed himself recommended eating a pomegranate in order to purge oneself of envy and hatred. Chicken braised with pomegranate juice and walnuts is one of the great dishes of Iranian cuisine. With vegetables, the juice provides the essential tang that balances a sweet glaze. You may need to look for pomegranate juice in food stores specializing in Middle Eastern products, or in the juice department of health food stores.

YIELD: 4 SERVINGS

5 TO 6 MEDIUM CARROTS
3 TABLESPOONS UNSALTED BUTTER, OR TO TASTE
1½ TEASPOONS POTATO STARCH
½ CUP BOTTLED POMEGRANATE JUICE
HONEY

Peel the carrots and cut into sticks. Melt the butter in a skillet, add the carrots and cook, tightly covered, until tender, about 45 minutes. Add more butter if desired.

Stir the potato starch into the juice in a bowl until smooth, and sweeten to taste with honey. Combine the sauce with the butter-cooked carrots and heat, stirring, until the sauce thickens and the carrots are well coated.

Variation: *Use the same sauce on small whole beets or sliced beets.*

Chunky Vegetable Salad with Herb Dressing

Fresh herbs brighten the low-fat dressing in this salad.

YIELD: 6 SERVINGS AS A SIDE DISH

4 CUPS VEGETABLES (CHERRY TOMATOES, CUCUMBER, ASPARAGUS, COOKED BEETS, POTATOES, LETTUCE, MIXED GREENS, OR A COMBINATION), CUT INTO $\frac{3}{4}$-INCH CHUNKS

1 TABLESPOON MILD HONEY

$\frac{1}{2}$ TABLESPOON FRESHLY SQUEEZED LEMON JUICE, OR MORE TO TASTE

$\frac{1}{2}$ CUP PLAIN YOGURT

1 TABLESPOON SCALLIONS, MINCED

1 TABLESPOON PARSLEY, MINCED

1 TEASPOON FRESH OREGANO, DILL, CHERVIL, OR BASIL, MINCED

$\frac{1}{2}$ TEASPOON SALT

Place cut vegetables in a serving bowl. In a small bowl, combine the honey and lemon juice. Stir in yogurt, herbs, and salt. Mix with the vegetables and serve.

BORSCHT WITH SOUR CHERRIES

Cold soups are commonplace in European homes, and they deserve attention from anyone who would like more choices for beginning a meal. This version of borscht has something special added: sour cherries, dyed purple by the beet juice. Serve with sour cream as a first course.

YIELD: 6 SERVINGS

5 TO 6 SMALL FRESH BEETS, GRATED OR THINLY SLICED
1 ONION, THINLY SLICED
1 CAN (15- OR 16-OUNCE) SOUR RED CHERRIES, DRAINED
3 WHOLE CLOVES
2 TABLESPOONS MILD HONEY
2 TABLESPOONS FRESHLY SQUEEZED LEMON JUICE
SALT

Cook the beets and onion in 5 cups water for about 30 minutes. Simmer the cherries with the cloves in 1 cup water for 5 minutes. Drain the beets, discarding the pulp, and combine the strained liquid with the cherries and their liquid. Season with honey, lemon juice, and salt to taste. Adjust seasoning so the sweet-and-sour balance subtly enhances the other flavors.

BROILED PINEAPPLE

YIELD: 8 SERVINGS

1 FRESH PINEAPPLE, PARED, CORED, AND CUT INTO CHUNKS, OR 1 CAN (20 OUNCES)
   UNSWEETENED PINEAPPLE, WELL DRAINED
HONEY TO TASTE

Preheat broiler. Spread the pineapple chunks in an even layer in a broiler-proof serving dish. Drizzle lightly and evenly with honey. Broil 6 inches from the heat for about 10 minutes, until bubbling and slightly browned at the edges. Spoon into dessert cups and serve hot.

SWEET-AND-SOUR COLE SLAW

In New Hampshire, cider vinegar has long been enjoyed for its flavor and for its reputation as a cure-all. Often used liberally on cooked parsnips and fresh cucumber slices, in this slaw it makes a particularly pleasing sweet-and-sour combination with the honey. Try this slaw served in side dishes with a meal of baked beans, hot dogs, and cornbread as they do in New Hampshire.

YIELD: 8 SERVINGS OR MORE

1 LARGE HEAD CABBAGE (ABOUT 2 POUNDS), QUARTERED, CORED, AND SHREDDED
2 YELLOW ONIONS, PEELED AND SLICED PAPER THIN
¼ CUP SUGAR
¼ CUP MILD HONEY
2 TEASPOONS FIRMLY PACKED BROWN SUGAR
1 TABLESPOON SALT
1 TEASPOON DRY MUSTARD
⅔ CUP BLAND OIL
1 CUP APPLE CIDER VINEGAR
1 TEASPOON CELERY SEEDS

Place the cabbage in a very large bowl and arrange the onion slices on top of the cabbage. Sprinkle with the sugar and drizzle with the honey, without stirring.

Combine the brown sugar, salt, dry mustard, oil, vinegar, and celery seed in a small saucepan and bring to a boil. Pour over the cabbage and onions. Stir everything together and let sit at least 4 hours.

NOTE: As the slaw marinates, its apparent volume will shrink by at least a half. Transfer to a glass serving dish and store, covered, in the refrigerator. Use as needed. It will keep 2 weeks.

TOMATO SHERBET IN AVOCADO CUPS

Honey enhances the fresh tomato flavor without making it unnaturally sweet and creates this extraordinarily tasty and beautiful sherbet.

YIELD: 4 SERVINGS

8 LARGE RIPE TOMATOES
3 TABLESPOONS FRESHLY SQUEEZED LEMON JUICE
1 TABLESPOON ONION JUICE (SEE NOTE)
2 TABLESPOONS MILD HONEY
½ TEASPOON GROUND FENNEL SEED
½ TEASPOON SALT
¼ TEASPOON PEPPER
4 AVOCADO HALVES
MINCED FRESH HERBS, FOR GARNISH

Peel, seed, and purée the tomatoes through the finest grate of a food mill. (If you cannot find ripe tomatoes, substitute top-quality tomato juice, reducing it by boiling until slightly thickened.) Add the lemon juice, onion juice, honey, fennel seed, salt, and pepper to the purée, and adjust the seasoning. Pour into a freezer tray, cover with plastic wrap, and freeze until quite firm. (If it has frozen solid, allow the sherbet to soften at room temperature for half an hour before serving.) Scoop the sherbet into the avocado halves and garnish with the herbs.

NOTE: To make onion juice, cut onion into chunks that will fit into a garlic press; squeeze.

Pickled Beets

Serve these beets as they are or arrange them in rows on a salad platter with slices of fresh garden cucumbers. Pass a separate bowl of yogurt.

YIELD: 6 SERVINGS

8 SMALL BEETS, BOILED AND PEELED
⅓ CUP RED WINE
¼ CUP TARRAGON WINE VINEGAR
2 TABLESPOONS MILD HONEY
1 TEASPOON GROUND CLOVES
1 TEASPOON GROUND CINNAMON
SALT
FRESHLY GROUND PEPPER

Slice the beets and place in a glass serving dish. Put the wine, vinegar, honey, cloves, cinnamon, and salt and pepper to taste in a small saucepan and bring to a boil. Cook 1 minute. Pour the marinade over the beets and stir to distribute evenly. Cool and then chill in the refrigerator for several hours.

MAIN
DISHES

LAMB BRAISED WITH FRUIT AND HONEY

Some of the outstanding dishes of Middle Eastern cooking are meats and fruits simmered until a rich sauce is formed, served with Persian rice or couscous. This tajine, a specialty of Fez, further heightens flavor by adding honey in the last minutes of cooking, but the sweetness is balanced by spices and pungent black pepper. Many variations on the dish are possible. This dish is best presented as one of several entrées in a meal of many courses.

YIELD: 6 SERVINGS

3 POUNDS LEG OF LAMB, CUT INTO 1-INCH CUBES

2 TABLESPOONS OIL

1/4 TEASPOON GROUND DRIED GINGER

1/2 TEASPOON GROUND CORIANDER

1 TEASPOON GROUND CINNAMON

1 TEASPOON SALT

1 TEASPOON FRESHLY GROUND BLACK PEPPER, OR MORE AS NEEDED

1 ONION, FINELY CHOPPED

3 GREEN APPLES, PEELED AND CUT INTO CHUNKS

2 TABLESPOONS HONEY

TOASTED SESAME SEEDS, FOR GARNISH

Place the lamb, oil, ginger, coriander, cinnamon, salt, pepper, and onion in a heavy stove-to-oven casserole. Add water almost to the level of the meat. Bring to a boil, cover, and simmer very gently for 2 hours. If the sauce is thin, drain it from the pot and place in a large shallow pan. Boil rapidly to reduce to about 2 cups. Return the sauce to the meat, add the chunks of apple, and simmer 20 minutes. (They will cook in the steam. Watch out that they do not get mushy.) A few minutes before the apples are soft, add the honey. Taste the sauce and reseason, adding more salt and freshly ground pepper as required. (Season highly, because the sauce will not taste as strong when eaten with the meat and rice.) Serve at once, sprinkled with the sesame seeds.

Variation: Instead of the apples, add $^1/_2$ pound prunes and finish as directed. This should cook down to a thick, rich sauce. Or you could substitute about $^1/_4$ teaspoon saffron for the coriander. Instead of the apples, you could use well-drained sour red cherries. When they are tender, mash the cherries with the back of a spoon so they further blend into the sauce.

HONEY-MUSTARD GLAZE

YIELD: GLAZE FOR 1 BRISKET

2 TABLESPOONS DIJON MUSTARD
$^1/_4$ CUP HONEY
2 TABLESPOONS FIRMLY PACKED BROWN SUGAR

Combine the mustard, honey, and brown sugar in a small saucepan and bring to a boil. Reduce the heat and simmer about 5 minutes, stirring frequently. Preheat broiler. Place a cooked corned beef brisket or a thick slice of ham on a broiler rack and brush with the glaze. Broil 6 inches from the heat for 10 minutes, brushing twice with additional glaze. Serve at once.

Marinade for Lamb

YIELD: 6 SERVINGS

½ CUP HONEY
¼ CUP FRESHLY SQUEEZED LEMON JUICE
¼ CUP WORCESTERSHIRE SAUCE
¼ CUP DRY SHERRY
GROUND DRIED GINGER
SALT
PEPPER

Combine the honey, lemon juice, Worcestershire, and sherry. Rub the selected cut of lamb (riblets, chunks of boned meat, or round-bone chops) with ginger, salt, and pepper. Place in a ceramic bowl and cover with the marinade. Let stand at room temperature for 4 hours or refrigerate, covered, overnight. Grill the meat over charcoal or in the oven, brushing several times with additional marinade.

PINEAPPLE-GLAZED CHICKEN

YIELD: 6 SERVINGS

6 SKINLESS WHOLE CHICKEN BREASTS
$\frac{1}{2}$ CUP HONEY
1 TABLESPOON GROUND CINNAMON
$\frac{1}{2}$ TABLESPOON CURRY POWDER
1 TEASPOON SALT
1 CLOVE GARLIC, MINCED
$\frac{3}{4}$ CUP UNSWEETENED CANNED GRAPEFRUIT JUICE
1 CUP CRUSHED CANNED PINEAPPLE

Place the chicken breasts in a single layer in a large frying pan. Combine the honey, cinnamon, curry powder, salt, and garlic in a large measuring cup. Stir in the grapefruit juice, blending well. Pour over the chicken. Cover the pan and simmer over medium heat for 20 minutes, stirring to prevent sticking and turning the chicken once. Preheat the broiler. When the chicken is tender, transfer to a broiler-proof serving dish. Combine the pan juices with the pineapple and spread this mixture evenly over the chicken pieces.

Broil 6 inches from the heat for 5 minutes, or until lightly glazed and bubbling. Serve with steamed rice.

Lima Bean Casserole

1 POUND DRIED LIMA BEANS
3 STRIPS OF BACON
1 ONION, DICED
1 GREEN BELL PEPPER, DICED
1 CLOVE GARLIC, CRUSHED
1 TOMATO, DICED
3 TABLESPOONS HONEY
SALT
FRESHLY GROUND PEPPER

Soak the lima beans overnight in a large cooking pot in water to cover by 2 inches. Next day, simmer them in the water for 30 minutes. Preheat the oven to 350°. Fry the bacon, cut it into small pieces, and remove from the pan, leaving the fat. Sauté the bell pepper, garlic, and tomato gently in the bacon fat until soft. Remove from the heat, stir in the honey, and add salt and pepper to taste.

Lift the lima beans from the cooking liquid and add to the skillet, mixing all together. Pour into a 1½-quart baking dish, adding liquid to come almost to the top of the beans. Taste for seasoning, using enough pepper so that the dish is spicy. Bake about 40 minutes, adding liquid if needed. In the final 5 minutes, top with the reserved bacon bits and serve at once.

Savory Soybeans

These protein-rich baked soybeans are nice to serve with Squash Cornbread (page 46) and a fresh cucumber-yogurt salad. The beans improve in flavor if made in advance and reheated.

YIELD: 6 SERVINGS

1½ CUPS DRIED SOYBEANS
2 SMALL TOMATOES, CHOPPED
½ CUP TOMATO SAUCE
1 SMALL GREEN BELL PEPPER, SEEDED AND CHOPPED
3 GREEN ONIONS, CHOPPED, INCLUDING THE TOPS
3 SLICES BACON, DICED
3 TABLESPOONS HONEY
1 TABLESPOON DRY MUSTARD
1 TEASPOON SALT (OR MORE IF PREFERRED)
FRESHLY GROUND PEPPER

Place the soybeans in a 3-quart kettle. Add water to 1 inch above the beans. Cover and soak overnight. The next day, drain the beans, discarding any loose husks, and return them to the kettle. Preheat the oven to 325°. Combine the beans with the remaining ingredients, adding water to barely cover. Bring to a boil on top of the stove, cover, then place the pan in the oven and bake for 4 hours, until tender. (The beans should be a tawny color, the liquid reduced by half. If you prefer dryer beans, bake another hour.)

Pork Loin Roasted with Orange and Ginger

YIELD: 6 SERVINGS

1 LOIN OF PORK (4 TO 5 POUNDS)
2 TEASPOONS SALT
FRESHLY GROUND PEPPER
1 CUP FRESHLY SQUEEZED ORANGE JUICE
⅓ CUP HONEY
1 TABLESPOON GROUND DRIED GINGER
¼ TEASPOON GROUND CLOVES

Preheat the oven to 325°. Rub the pork roast with salt and pepper to taste and place fat side up in a roasting pan. Cook 1½ to 3 hours, or until a meat thermometer placed in the flesh of the roast reaches 180°.

Combine the orange juice, honey, ginger, and cloves in a small saucepan and simmer 30 minutes. During the last hour of cooking, brush the roast several times with this mixture to produce a shiny glaze. Serve with rice pilaf or black beans.

Opposite page: Pork Loin Roasted wuth Orange and Ginger (above), and Fresh Corn Cakes with Honey (page 74).

Fresh Corn Cakes with Honey

Serve these cakes hot from the pan, with dollops of crème fraîche sprinkled with cilantro. Pass honey at the table to drizzle over the cakes.

YIELD: 4 GENEROUS SERVINGS

3 OR 4 EARS FRESH CORN
2 EGGS
½ CUP WHOLE MILK
2 TABLESPOONS UNSALTED BUTTER, MELTED AND COOLED
¼ CUP UNBLEACHED WHITE FLOUR
½ CUP YELLOW CORNMEAL
1 TEASPOON SALT
FRESHLY GROUND PEPPER

TOPPINGS
¾ CUP CRÈME FRAÎCHE
¼ CUP CHOPPED FRESH CILANTRO
TABLE HONEY, SUCH AS ALFALFA OR BLACKBERRY

Cut the kernels from the corn with a sharp knife and place in a food processor or blender. Pulse about 4 times, or whiz briefly if using the blender. (The corn should be coarsely chopped with some liquid. Measure off 1½ cups and use the remainder for something else.) In a medium bowl, whisk together the eggs, milk, and butter. Add the corn, flour, cornmeal, salt, and season with pepper to taste.

Heat a large, heavy frying pan or griddle and coat lightly with oil. Make small cakes with a large spoonful of the mixture and fry until golden, about 2 minutes. Turn and fry the other side until golden.

CORN FRITTERS

Serve these fritters hot with additional honey. A pleasant accompaniment to pork sausages or Canadian bacon, for either brunch or supper.

YIELD: 16 TO 20 FRITTERS (ABOUT 4 SERVINGS)

1 PACKAGE (10 OUNCES) FROZEN CORN
1 TABLESPOON UNSALTED BUTTER
1/4 CUP WHOLE MILK
1 EGG
1/2 CUP UNBLEACHED WHITE FLOUR
1/2 TEASPOON BAKING POWDER
1/2 TEASPOON SALT
FRESHLY GROUND PEPPER
1 TEASPOON HONEY
1 TO 2 TEASPOONS SNIPPED FRESH CHIVES
VEGETABLE SHORTENING FOR FRYING
TABLE HONEY, SUCH AS ALFALFA OR BLACKBERRY

Place the frozen corn, 1 tablespoon of water, and the butter in a saucepan that can be tightly covered. Bring to a boil over high heat. Decrease the heat, add the milk, cover, and simmer until tender, about 5 minutes. Drain and cool, reserving the liquid.

Beat the egg in a small bowl and add the flour, baking powder, salt, pepper to taste, honey, and the reserved corn milk. Stir in 1 1/2 cups of the corn and the snipped chives.

Heat the shortening in a large frying pan, allowing 1-inch depth. Place the batter in the pan by the tablespoonful, allowing ample space so that crowding does not prevent even cooking. Add liquid or flour as needed to make lacy cakes. Fry until brown and crisp, about 3 minutes, turn, and transfer to paper towels to drain.

Caramelized Honey and Herb Sauce

Sweet and pungent, this sauce is delicious with sautéed pork chops, duck, or turkey thighs.

YIELD: 6 SERVINGS

¼ CUP MILD HONEY, SUCH AS CLOVER
1 (2-INCH) SPRIG OF FRESH THYME OR SAVORY
¼ CUP RED WINE VINEGAR
½ CUP CHICKEN OR VEGETABLE STOCK
SALT
PEPPER

Combine the honey and thyme in a small, heavy saucepan. Over low heat, bring to a boil and cook to a deep golden brown, about 10 minutes. Watch carefully to avoid scorching. Remove from the heat, add the vinegar and stock and stir to combine. Back on the stove, raise the heat until the mixture boils, then cook over medium heat until thickened, about 15 minutes.

COOKIES
and
CAKES

Fat Honey Cookies

It is always nice to have on hand a simple, delicious cookie that will please a child or make a filling snack. These spice cookies are good candidates for the perpetual jar because they contain little sugar, keep remarkably well because of the honey, and are easily mixed and shaped.

YIELD: 4 DOZEN COOKIES

4 CUPS UNBLEACHED WHITE FLOUR
1½ TEASPOONS SALT
1 TEASPOON BAKING SODA
1 TEASPOON BAKING POWDER
2 TEASPOONS GROUND CINNAMON
2 TEASPOONS GROUND DRIED GINGER
½ TEASPOON GROUND CLOVES
1 CUP UNSALTED BUTTER
1¼ CUPS MILD HONEY, SUCH AS CLOVER
¼ CUP SUGAR
1 EGG

Sift the flour with the salt, soda, baking powder, and spices, and set aside. Melt the butter over low heat with the honey and sugar in a saucepan large enough to hold the complete recipe. Cool to lukewarm. Beat in the egg. Add the flour mixture in several additions, beating briefly. (If the dough is not easy to handle, chill it.) Preheat the oven to 350°. Lightly grease baking sheets. Shape the cookies by rolling in your palms to 1½-inch balls. Place the cookies on the baking sheets about 2 inches apart. (One dozen fits well on a large baking sheet.) Bake 15 minutes, until lightly browned. Remove from the pans at once and transfer to racks to cool. Store in airtight tins.

CRISPY WALNUT COOKIES

Here is a basic formula for crisp cookies, not very sweet and easy to make.

YIELD: ABOUT 3 DOZEN COOKIES

1 CUP WHOLE-WHEAT FLOUR
½ TEASPOON BAKING SODA
½ TEASPOON SALT
⅓ CUP UNSALTED BUTTER, MELTED
⅜ CUP HONEY
½ TEASPOON VANILLA EXTRACT
1 EGG
1 CUP CHOPPED WALNUTS OR OTHER NUTS

Sift flour, soda, and salt together into a mixing bowl. Combine the butter, honey, and vanilla and stir into the flour mixture. Preheat the oven to 375°. Add the egg, mix into the batter, and stir in the walnuts. Drop by the teaspoonful on an ungreased baking sheet. Bake about 10 minutes, until lightly browned. Transfer to racks to cool.

PEANUT BUTTER COOKIES

YIELD: 3 DOZEN COOKIES

1¼ CUPS UNBLEACHED WHITE FLOUR
½ TEASPOON BAKING POWDER
¾ TEASPOON BAKING SODA
¼ TEASPOON SALT
¼ CUP BUTTER
½ CUP CRUNCHY PEANUT BUTTER
½ CUP SUGAR
½ CUP MILD HONEY
1 EGG

Sift the flour, baking powder, soda, and salt into a small bowl and set aside. In a large bowl, beat the butter, peanut butter, sugar, honey, and egg until well blended. Add the dry ingredients and mix thoroughly. Cover and chill 2 hours.

Preheat the oven to 375°. Grease baking sheets lightly. Roll bits of dough into walnut-sized balls and place 2 inches apart on baking sheets. Flatten with a fork dipped in flour, making a criss-cross pattern. Bake 10 to 12 minutes. Allow the cookies to rest on the pan a minute before transferring to a rack to cool rack.

ITALIAN PINE NUT COOKIES

Pine nuts are native only to the western part of the United States, but they are plentiful in Italy, southern France, and the Middle East, where they are widely used in sweets and pilafs and meat dishes. These cookies are delicate in flavor, just the thing to follow a pasta meal.

YIELD: ABOUT 2 DOZEN COOKIES

½ CUP UNSALTED BUTTER, ROOM TEMPERATURE
1 TABLESPOON SUGAR
2 TABLESPOONS MILD HONEY
1 CUP UNBLEACHED WHITE FLOUR
2 TEASPOONS BRANDY
½ CUP PINE NUTS

Preheat the oven to 375°. Lightly grease baking sheets. Cream the butter, incorporating the sugar and honey. Mix in the flour and brandy, and then the pine nuts. Shape by the teaspoonful into small balls with the palms of your hands. Place on baking sheets 1 inch apart. (They will spread slightly but remain uniformly round.) Bake 10 minutes, until pale gold. Transfer to racks to cool.

GERMAN CHRISTMAS COOKIES

Spicy cookies and cakes have been made in Northern Europe since the early days of trading with Asia. Fragrant with cinnamon, cloves, cardamom, mace, nutmeg, coriander, and embellished with the peels of oranges, lemons, and citron, these delicacies became part of holiday celebrations, taking on characteristics of particular countries as recipes were refined and handed down through the generations. The honey and spices, both natural preservatives, combine to make cookies that can be stored for months, and in fact mellow and improve in flavor and texture from the aging process. Although they are associated with winter and the holidays, honey-spice cookies are tasty with a dish of fruit in any season. These Christmas cookies in the German style are the recipe of a friend who always makes them at Christmas, just as her mother always did.

YIELD: ABOUT 6 DOZEN COOKIES

2¾ CUPS UNBLEACHED WHITE FLOUR

1 TEASPOON GROUND CINNAMON

1 TEASPOON GROUND CLOVES

1 TEASPOON ALLSPICE

1 TEASPOON FRESHLY GRATED NUTMEG

½ CUP HONEY

½ CUP MOLASSES

¾ CUP FIRMLY PACKED BROWN SUGAR

1 EGG, BEATEN

1 TABLESPOON FRESHLY SQUEEZED LEMON JUICE

GRATED RIND OF 1 LEMON

⅓ CUP CITRON, OR CANDIED ORANGE PEEL (PAGE 54), CHOPPED

⅓ CUP CHOPPED WALNUTS OR ALMONDS

GLAZE
½ CUP CONFECTIONERS' SUGAR
2 TABLESPOONS CORNSTARCH
½ TEASPOON VANILLA EXTRACT OR BRANDY
1 TO 3 TABLESPOONS HOT WATER

Sift the flour with spices and set aside. Heat the honey, molasses, and brown sugar to a boil in a large, heavy saucepan. Cool to lukewarm. Stir in the egg and lemon juice. Grate the lemon rind directly into the pan so that no aromatic oils are lost. Stir in the flour mixture in several additions, mixing thoroughly. Work in the citron and nuts. Cover and chill 12 hours or more.

Preheat the oven to 400° and lightly grease baking sheets. On a floured board, roll the dough ¼ inch thick, a small amount at a time. Keep the remainder refrigerated. Cut into rectangles 1½ by 2½ inches. Place 1 inch apart on the baking sheets to allow for spreading. Bake 10 to 12 minutes, until the edges have browned.

To prepare the glaze, combine the confectioners' sugar, cornstarch, vanilla, and just enough hot water to make a smooth thick paste. Transfer the cookies to a wire rack and brush with glaze while hot. Cool thoroughly.

NOTE: Store the cookies in airtight tins and age several days before eating. The cookies will keep for months.

Swiss Holiday Spice Cookies

Swiss Holiday Spice Cookies, Leckerli in the style of Basel, should be baked several weeks or even months before they are needed. Once they have cooled they become hard, and it takes weeks to develop a fine texture. A piece of bread or wedge of apple can be stored in the tin with them to hasten the softening.

YIELD: ABOUT 8 DOZEN COOKIES

1¼ CUPS HONEY

⅓ CUP KIRSCH

1 CUP SUGAR

GRATED RIND OF 1 LEMON

¼ CUP CHOPPED CANDIED LEMON PEEL (PAGE 54)

¼ CUP CHOPPED CANDIED ORANGE PEEL (PAGE 54)

1 CUP BLANCHED ALMONDS, GRATED (SEE NOTE)

4 CUPS UNBLEACHED WHITE FLOUR

1 TABLESPOON GROUND CINNAMON

1 TEASPOON GROUND NUTMEG

½ TEASPOON GROUND CLOVES

PINCH OF SALT

1 TEASPOON BAKING SODA

GLAZE

½ CUP CONFECTIONERS' SUGAR

2 TABLESPOONS CORNSTARCH

½ TEASPOON VANILLA EXTRACT OR BRANDY

1 TO 3 TABLESPOONS HOT WATER

Bring the honey to a boil in a large saucepan, watching carefully (like milk, it can bolt). Remove from the heat and stir in the kirsch and the sugar. Return to low heat and stir until the sugar has melted. Cool. Grate the lemon rind directly into the pan so that no aromatic oils will be lost, and add fruit peels. Stir in the almonds.

Sift together the flour, spices, salt, and baking soda. Stir this into the saucepan. Add flour as required to make a dough that will clear the sides of the pan. Cover and ripen in a cool place overnight, several days, or a week.

To roll out, preheat the oven to 325°, butter baking sheets heavily, and dust them with flour. Roll the dough ¼ inch thick on a lightly floured surface and cut into rectangles. Place close together on the baking pans and bake 20 to 25 minutes, until uniformly golden. Transfer to racks to cool.

To prepare the glaze, combine the sugar, cornstarch, vanilla, and just enough water to make a smooth paste. Transfer the cookies to a rack and brush with glaze while warm.

NOTE: Chop almonds, place in work bowl of a food processor, and process until a fine, dry meal is formed (1 to 2 minutes). Store the cookies in airtight tins and age several weeks before serving. The cookies will keep for months.

POLISH CHRISTMAS TREE COOKIES

YIELD: 6 DOZEN MEDIUM COOKIES, SUCH AS 3-INCH STARS

½ CUP UNSALTED BUTTER

1 CUP SUGAR

1 CUP HONEY

2 TABLESPOONS HEAVY WHIPPING CREAM

1 TABLESPOON GROUND CINNAMON

1½ TEASPOONS GROUND DRIED GINGER

½ TEASPOON GROUND CLOVES

¼ TEASPOON FRESHLY GRATED NUTMEG

GRATED RIND OF 1 LEMON

3½ TO 4 CUPS UNBLEACHED WHITE FLOUR PLUS ADDITIONAL AS NEEDED

Grease and flour baking sheets. Cream the butter with the sugar until light and fluffy. Add the honey, cream, spices, and blend thoroughly. Grate the lemon rind directly into the bowl so that no aromatic oils are lost. Sift the flour and add it gradually to the butter mixture, beating well after each addition, until the dough is stiff enough to roll. Chill briefly.

Preheat the oven to 350°. Roll out the dough ⅛ inch thick on a floured surface and cut into desired shapes. (The dough may be sticky.) Transfer the cookies carefully to the baking sheets and bake 10 minutes, or until just beginning to brown around the edges. Transfer to a rack to cool. Store in an airtight jar.

NOTE: To make cookies sturdy enough to hang on a Christmas tree, add up to ½ cup additional flour to make a stiffer dough. Before baking, make a small hole in each cookie with the tip of a paring knife. When cool, ice the cookies with white icing and candies, string yarn through the holes, and tie on tree branches.

Nutmeg Coconut Squares

YIELD: 16 COOKIES

1 CUP CAKE FLOUR
PINCH OF SALT
1/8 TEASPOON BAKING SODA
1/2 CUP SUGAR
1/4 CUP UNSALTED BUTTER, MELTED
1/2 TEASPOON FRESHLY GRATED NUTMEG
1/4 CUP MILD HONEY
2 EGG WHITES
1 TABLESPOON WHOLE MILK
3/4 CUP MOIST SHREDDED COCONUT

Preheat the oven to 350°. Butter heavily an 8-inch square pan and line with waxed paper cut to fit the bottom of the pan. Sift the cake flour, salt, soda, and sugar into a mixing bowl. Stir in the remaining ingredients until thoroughly mixed, without overbeating. Pour into the pan and bake 35 minutes, until the top is firm to a gentle touch. Remove from the pan, remove the waxed paper, and transfer to a rack to cool. Cut into squares. Store in airtight tins. Age 24 hours before serving. (Flavor improves with longer storage.)

Honey Nut Crumbcake

This coffeecake lends itself to a two-stage preparation. The dry crumb mixture can be mixed ahead of time and the buttermilk, honey, and egg set out to be combined quickly so that you are half an hour away from fresh, hot bread whenever you want it. Portions can be wrapped in foil and reheated in a 350° oven.

YIELD: 12 SERVINGS

¾ CUP UNSALTED BUTTER, AT ROOM TEMPERATURE

1 CUP FIRMLY PACKED LIGHT BROWN SUGAR

½ TEASPOON SALT

½ TEASPOON GROUND CINNAMON

½ TEASPOON FRESHLY GRATED NUTMEG

2¼ CUPS UNBLEACHED WHITE FLOUR

¾ CUP BROKEN WALNUTS

1 TEASPOON BAKING SODA

½ TEASPOON BAKING POWDER

1 CUP BUTTERMILK

¾ CUP MILD HONEY

1 EGG

Preheat the oven to 350°. Grease a 9 by 13-inch baking pan. Cream together the butter and brown sugar in a large mixing bowl. Add the salt, cinnamon, nutmeg, and flour, mixing with your fingertips until uniform, non-sticky crumbs are formed. Set aside ½ cup of this mixture and add the walnuts to it; this will be the topping. To the other half of the mixture, add the soda and baking powder. In a large measuring cup, combine the buttermilk, honey, and egg. Stir into the flour mixture until all ingredients are moist. Spread in the prepared pan and sprinkle the reserved nut crumbs over the top, pressing in gently. Bake 25 to 30 minutes, until top springs back when gently pressed and cake has begun to shrink from the sides of the pan. Serve warm, cut directly from the pan.

Upside-Down Apple Cake

A shiny lemon glaze distinguishes this apple cake, nice to make during the long months when other fruits are in short supply. Serve warm, either plain or with whipped cream sweetened with a touch of honey.

YIELD: ONE 10-INCH ROUND CAKE

2 GENEROUS CUPS TART GREEN APPLES (ABOUT 3), PEELED AND SLICED
$\frac{1}{3}$ CUP MILD HONEY
$\frac{1}{8}$ TEASPOON FRESHLY GRATED NUTMEG
GRATED RIND OF 1 LEMON
JUICE OF 1 LEMON
1 TABLESPOON PLUS 1 CUP UNBLEACHED WHITE FLOUR
2 TABLESPOONS UNSALTED BUTTER
$\frac{1}{2}$ CUP SUGAR
1 TEASPOON BAKING POWDER
$\frac{1}{4}$ TEASPOON SALT
$\frac{1}{4}$ CUP MILK
1 EGG PLUS 1 EGG YOLK
1 TABLESPOON UNSALTED BUTTER, MELTED

Butter heavily a 10-inch glass pie plate. Place slices of apples in a large bowl. Combine the honey, nutmeg, lemon rind, lemon juice, and 1 tablespoon of the flour and pour over the apples, stirring well to coat all the pieces. Arrange the apple slices in neat circles on the bottom of the pie plate, pouring any of the honey mixture left in the bowl over them. Dot with the 2 tablespoons of butter.

    Preheat the oven to 425°. Sift together the remaining flour, sugar, baking powder, and salt into a mixing bowl. In a measuring cup, combine the milk, egg and yolk, and melted butter. Add to the dry ingredients and stir until blended. Carefully spread the batter over the apples. Bake 25 to 30 minutes until the top is browned and the fruit is golden and bubbly. Cool in the pan a few minutes, then reverse onto a platter before the honey glaze hardens.

Mrs. G's Chocolate Brownies

A recipe from a dear New Hampshire lady who always treats visitors to an astounding array of home-made goodies.

YIELD: 16 BROWNIES

½ CUP UNBLEACHED WHITE FLOUR
½ TEASPOON BAKING POWDER
¼ TEASPOON SALT
6 OUNCES (6 SQUARES) SEMISWEET CHOCOLATE
⅓ CUP VEGETABLE SHORTENING
2 EGGS, BEATEN
6 TABLESPOONS MILD HONEY
1 TEASPOON VANILLA EXTRACT
1 CUP WALNUTS OR PECANS, CHOPPED

Preheat the oven to 350°. Butter an 8-inch square pan. Sift the flour, baking powder, and salt into a small bowl. Set aside. Melt the chocolate and shortening in a double boiler over warm, not boiling, water. Remove from the heat and beat in the eggs, honey, and vanilla. Stir in the dry ingredients and nuts, and beat until well blended. Spread in the prepared pan and bake 25 to 30 minutes. Cool in the pan and cut into squares.

NOTE: These are cake-like in texture, but Mrs. G. says, "If the chewy kind is preferred, take it out of the oven before it is really done."

Opposite page, from left: Swiss Holiday Spice Cookies (pages 84–85), Mrs. G's Chocolate Brownies (above), and Italian Pine Nut Cookies (page 81).

Christmas Gingerbread Loaf

YIELD: ONE 9-INCH SQUARE CAKE, OR 9 SERVINGS

GINGERBREAD
1/2 CUP DARK HONEY
1/2 TEASPOON GROUND DRIED GINGER
1/2 TEASPOON GROUND CINNAMON
1/2 TEASPOON GROUND CLOVES
1 1/4 CUPS UNBLEACHED WHITE FLOUR
1/2 TEASPOON BAKING POWDER
1/2 TEASPOON BAKING SODA
1/4 TEASPOON SALT
1/4 CUP UNSALTED BUTTER
1/4 CUP FIRMLY PACKED BROWN SUGAR
GRATED RIND OF 1/2 A LEMON
1 EGG
1/2 CUP BUTTERMILK

LEMON FILLING
1/4 CUP MILD HONEY
1 1/2 TABLESPOONS POTATO STARCH
1/8 TEASPOON SALT
1/3 CUP WATER
1 EGG YOLK
1/2 TABLESPOON UNSALTED BUTTER
GRATED RIND OF 2 LEMONS
5 TABLESPOONS FRESHLY SQUEEZED LEMON JUICE
2 CUPS HEAVY CREAM, WHIPPED AND SWEETENED
CANDIED LEMON PEEL (PAGE 54), FOR GARNISH

To prepare the gingerbread, grease a 9-inch square pan. In a small saucepan, combine the honey and spices, bring to a boil, remove from the heat, and cool. Preheat the oven to 350°. Sift the flour with the baking powder, soda, and salt and set aside. Cream the butter and brown sugar until light and fluffy. Add the cooled honey mixture and blend thoroughly. Grate the lemon rind directly into the bowl and add the egg, mixing until well blended. Add the flour mixture and buttermilk alternately, beating well after each addition. Pour into the prepared pan and bake 30 to 35 minutes, until a cake tester comes out clean. Cool in the pan 10 minutes, then transfer to a rack to cool completely.

To prepare the filling, combine the honey, potato starch, and salt in a small saucepan. Whisk the water in gradually. Bring to a boil, stirring constantly, and boil 1 minute. Remove from the heat and stir half of the mixture into the egg yolk, slightly beaten in a small bowl. Blend this mixture into the remaining syrup in the saucepan and boil 1 minute more. Remove from the heat, add the butter and lemon rind, and stir in the lemon juice gradually. Cool.

Cut the cooled cake in half horizontally and layer the halves with filling. Frost the entire loaf with the whipped cream. Decorate the top with flowerettes of candied lemon peel. Chill for 2 hours before serving.

NOTE: Store the filling in a covered jar in the refrigerator if not using immediately.

High Energy Snacks

Candy-like, these make an excellent addition to a child's lunch pail or to a backpack as a trail snack.

YIELD: ABOUT 1½ POUNDS

½ CUP CRUNCHY PEANUT BUTTER
¼ CUP HONEY
¼ CUP WATER
½ CUP NONFAT DRY MILK
½ CUP RAW WHEAT GERM
½ CUP SHREDDED UNSWEETENED COCONUT
½ CUP HULLED SUNFLOWER SEEDS, RAW OR TOASTED
½ CUP CHOPPED CASHEW NUTS, RAW OR TOASTED
½ CUP HULLED SESAME SEEDS

In a large bowl, combine all of the ingredients, stirring to create a thick, homogeneous mass. Press into a small buttered pan or roll into a log. Wrap and chill, then slice into rounds or cut into squares. Store in airtight containers.

Greek Walnut Cake

YIELD: ONE 8-INCH SQUARE CAKE

¹/₂ CUP UNBLEACHED WHITE FLOUR
¹/₂ CUP FARINA (REGULAR CREAM OF WHEAT)
¹/₂ CUP FINELY CHOPPED WALNUTS
1¹/₂ TEASPOON BAKING POWDER
¹/₂ TEASPOON GROUND CINNAMON
GRATED RIND OF ¹/₂ AN ORANGE
¹/₂ CUP UNSALTED BUTTER
¹/₂ CUP SUGAR
3 EGGS
³/₄ CUP BASIC HONEY SYRUP FOR PASTRIES (PAGE 126)

Preheat the oven to 350°. Grease an 8-inch square pan with oil. In a small bowl, combine the flour, farina, walnuts, baking powder, and cinnamon. Grate the orange rind directly into the bowl so no aromatic oils are lost. Set aside. In a large bowl, cream the butter and sugar until light and fluffy. Add the eggs one at a time, beating constantly. Add the dry ingredients in two parts and mix thoroughly. Pour into the pan and bake for 30 minutes. Remove the pan to a rack. Pour about ³/₄ cup cooled honey syrup over the warm cake, being careful to soak every part of it. Cool. Cut into squares or diamonds to serve.

Fresh Ginger Cake

This contemporary version of an old favorite is flavored with fresh ginger rather than the dried spice. Yogurt or sour cream is good alongside this cake, as are sliced peaches or fresh berries mixed with a little honey.

YIELD: 9 SERVINGS

½ CUP UNSALTED BUTTER, MELTED

½ CUP SOUR CREAM

½ CUP BUCKWHEAT HONEY

½ CUP SUGAR

2 EGGS

GRATED RIND OF 1 LEMON

4 TEASPOONS PEELED AND FINELY GRATED FRESH GINGER

2 CUPS UNBLEACHED WHITE FLOUR

1 TEASPOON BAKING SODA

½ TEASPOON SALT

Preheat the oven to 350°. Grease an 8-inch square pan. In a medium bowl, combine the butter, sour cream, honey, sugar, eggs, lemon rind, and ginger. Stir until smooth. Sift in the flour, soda, and salt. Stir to combine and spread in the baking pan. Bake until a tester comes out clean, 30 to 35 minutes. Cool briefly and turn out onto a rack, or cut and serve from the pan.

CHOCOLATE CUPCAKES

YIELD: 8 MEDIUM CUPCAKES

1 CUP CAKE FLOUR
1/4 TEASPOON SALT
1/4 TEASPOON BAKING SODA
3/4 TEASPOON BAKING POWDER
3 TABLESPOONS PLUS 1/2 CUP MILD HONEY
1/3 CUP WHOLE MILK
2 TABLESPOONS WATER
2 OUNCES GERMAN'S SWEET CHOCOLATE
1/4 CUP UNSALTED BUTTER
1 EGG
1/2 TEASPOON VANILLA EXTRACT

Grease and flour a cupcake pan or line with paper cups. Sift together the flour, salt, soda, and baking powder. Set aside. Preheat the oven to 375°.

In a small, heavy saucepan, combine the 3 tablespoons of honey, milk, water, and chocolate. Stir over very low heat until the chocolate is melted and the mixture is well blended. Cool.

Cream the butter until fluffy. Add the remaining honey in a thin stream, beating constantly. When the mixture is light and smooth, add the egg and vanilla, blending well. Alternately, add the dry ingredients and the chocolate mixture, beginning and ending with the dry ingredients. Mix just until smooth. Fill each pan two-thirds full and bake 18 to 20 minutes, until a cake tester in the center comes out clean. Remove from pan and transfer to a rack to cool.

Moist Lemon Cake

YIELD: 1 LOAF, OR 8 SERVINGS

½ CUP UNSALTED BUTTER
¼ CUP HONEY
½ CUP SUGAR
3 EGGS, SEPARATED
GRATED RIND OF 1 LEMON
½ CUP PLAIN LOWFAT YOGURT
½ TABLESPOON FRESHLY SQUEEZED LEMON JUICE
1½ CUPS UNBLEACHED WHITE FLOUR
1½ CUPS WHOLE-WHEAT PASTRY FLOUR
2 TEASPOONS BAKING POWDER
PINCH OF SALT

Preheat the oven to 350°. Butter an 8 by 4-inch baking pan. Cream together the butter, honey, and ¼ cup of the sugar. Beat in the egg yolks. Grate the lemon rind directly into the bowl so that no aromatic oils are lost, and add the yogurt and lemon juice. Sift together the flours, baking powder, and salt. Mix into the creamed ingredients in two additions. Beat the egg whites with the remaining ¼ cup of sugar until glossy, and fold in gently. Pour into the prepared pan.

Bake 1 hour, or until browned. (Reduce the heat if the loaf is browning too rapidly.) Cake is done when a tester in the center comes out clean. Cool in the pan, then remove and wrap well to store. The loaf will keep 2 or 3 days.

Traditional Jewish Honey Cake

YIELD: 1 LOAF, ABOUT 10 SERVINGS

1¾ CUP SIFTED UNBLEACHED WHITE FLOUR
⅛ TEASPOON SALT
¾ TEASPOON BAKING POWDER
½ TEASPOON BAKING SODA
¼ TEASPOON GROUND CINNAMON
¼ TEASPOON DRIED GROUND GINGER
⅛ TEASPOON NUTMEG, FRESHLY GRATED
⅛ TEASPOON GROUND CLOVES
2 EGGS
6 TABLESPOONS SUGAR
2 TABLESPOONS BLAND OIL
1 CUP HONEY
¼ CUP COLD COFFEE
¾ CUP CHOPPED WALNUTS

Grease a 9 by 5-inch loaf pan. Sift together the flour, salt, baking powder, baking soda, and spices and set aside. Preheat the oven to 325°.

Beat the eggs, then add the sugar gradually, beating until the mixture is thick and lemon-colored. Combine the oil, honey, and coffee in a large measuring cup and pour into the egg mixture. Blend well. Add the flour mixture and the nuts, stirring until all ingredients are moistened and the batter is smooth. Turn into the pan and bake 40 to 50 minutes, until nicely browned and a cake tester comes out clean. Cool in the pan 10 minutes before transferring to a rack to cool completely. Wrap well in plastic wrap and overwrap in foil. Age for one day to allow flavor to develop; the cake can be kept a week or two.

French Spice Loaf

YIELD: ONE 10 BY 5-INCH LOAF

Pain d'épice is a traditional French loaf tracing its antecedents back to the biblical breads of honey and flour. Although leavening and spices were added over time, the simple formula does not use butter or eggs. Buckwheat honey was used when plentiful, and the flavors of anise and orange are complementary to the dark honey. If using lighter honeys, try cinnamon, ginger, and nutmeg instead. In Dijon, where pain d'épice is a regional specialty, the batter is aged before baking. I like to let it stand overnight, but it can be baked after resting for just 10 minutes.

1 CUP DARK HONEY, SUCH AS BUCKWHEAT

½ CUP SUGAR

1 CUP HOT WATER

2 TEASPOONS BAKING SODA

1 TEASPOON BAKING POWDER

2 TEASPOONS ANISE SEED, CRUSHED

¼ TEASPOON SALT

½ TEASPOON DRY MUSTARD

GRATED RIND OF 1 ORANGE OR ¼ CUP CANDIED ORANGE PEEL (PAGE 54), CHOPPED

2 ¾ CUPS UNBLEACHED WHITE FLOUR

¾ CUP RYE FLOUR

HOT MILK, AS NEEDED

In a large bowl, combine the honey and sugar. Add the hot water and stir until smooth. Blend in the baking soda, baking powder, anise, salt, and mustard. Grate the orange rind directly into the bowl so no aromatic oils are lost. Add the flours one spoonful at a time, blending to a smooth batter. Set the batter in a cool place to stand for 10 minutes or overnight.

Preheat the oven to 350°. Pour the batter into a heavily buttered 10 by 5-inch loaf pan and bake 50 to 60 minutes, until a toothpick inserted in the middle comes out clean. Remove from oven and brush the loaf with hot milk. Cool in the pan for 10 minutes, then transfer to a rack to cool completely. Wrap well and age for a day or two before serving. The loaf will keep for weeks.

PIES
and
TARTS

PIE CRUST

YIELD: TWO 9-INCH PIE CRUSTS

2 CUPS UNBLEACHED WHITE FLOUR
1 TABLESPOON SUGAR
½ TEASPOON SALT
½ CUP VEGETABLE SHORTENING
3 TABLESPOONS BUTTER, CUT INTO SMALL PIECES
6 TO 7 TABLESPOONS ICE WATER

Put the flour into a medium bowl and stir in the sugar and salt. Cut the shortening and butter into the flour using a pastry blender until it resembles coarse meal. Sprinkle water over the surface and rub the dough together with your fingertips until it barely clings together in a ball. Add more water as needed. Turn the dough out onto a piece of waxed paper, shaking off any excess flour or loose particles on top. Press together firmly and wrap in plastic wrap while preparing the filling.

   To roll out, divide the dough in half. Roll on a lightly floured board and fit into pans as desired.

West Coast Raisin Pie

YIELD: ONE 9-INCH PIE

Two crusts Pie Crust (page 102)
2 cups raisins
1 cup freshly squeezed orange juice
¼ cup freshly squeezed lemon juice
5 tablespoons honey
Pinch of salt
Grated rind of 1 orange
4 tablespoons potato starch flour
¾ cup cold water
2 tablespoons butter

Preheat the oven to 425°. In a medium saucepan, mix the raisins, juices, honey, and salt. Grate the orange rind directly into the pan so no aromatic oils are lost.

In a small bowl, dissolve the potato starch flour in the water and add to the saucepan. Cook over medium heat until thick and smooth (about 5 minutes), stirring constantly. Remove from the heat. Stir in the butter until blended. Set aside to cool.

Line a 9-inch pie plate with one crust and fill with the cooled raisin mixture. Cut vents in the other crust and fit it over the top, sealing the two crusts well. Bake 30 to 40 minutes, until golden brown.

New England Pumpkin Pie

YIELD: ONE 9-INCH PIE

1 CRUST PIE CRUST (PAGE 102)
6 TABLESPOONS LIGHT OR DARK HONEY
1 CUP LIGHT CREAM
2 CUPS UNSWEETENED PUMPKIN PURÉE
4 EGGS, BEATEN
1 TEASPOON GROUND CINNAMON
½ TEASPOON GROUND DRIED GINGER
½ TEASPOON MACE
½ TEASPOON GROUND CLOVES
¾ TEASPOON SALT

Preheat the oven to 450°. In a medium bowl, stir the honey into the light cream in a thin stream, then stir into the pumpkin purée. Add the eggs, which have been beaten together, and the seasonings. Pour into the prepared pie shell. Bake at 450° for 10 minutes, then reduce temperature to 325° and bake until filling is set, about 40 minutes. Serve with a wedge of New Hampshire Cheddar cheese or with spiced whipped cream.

Deep South Sweet Potato Pie

YIELD: 6 SERVINGS

1 CRUST PIE CRUST (PAGE 102)
4 EGGS
6 TABLESPOONS HONEY
1 CUP HEAVY WHIPPING CREAM
1/3 CUP FRESHLY SQUEEZED ORANGE JUICE
PINCH OF SALT
1 TEASPOON VANILLA EXTRACT
1 1/2 CUPS MASHED COOKED YAMS
FRESHLY GRATED NUTMEG

Preheat the oven to 450°. Line a pie plate with the pastry, building up a fluted edge. Chill the crust while mixing the filling.

In a medium bowl, beat the eggs thoroughly. Stir in the honey, 2/3 cup of the cream, the orange juice, salt, and vanilla. Put the yams in a bowl and stir in the egg mixture until well mixed. Pour the filling into the crust and bake for 10 minutes. Decrease the heat to 350° and bake 30 minutes more, or until only the center jiggles when the pan is gently shaken. Let cool.

Whip the remaining cream and flavor with freshly grated nutmeg. Spread on top of the pie and serve.

SWEET TART PASTRY

YIELD: TWO 9-INCH TART SHELLS

2⅔ CUPS UNBLEACHED WHITE FLOUR
¼ CUP SUGAR
PINCH OF SALT
GRATED RIND OF 1 LEMON
1 CUP COLD UNSALTED BUTTER
2 EGG YOLKS

Place the flour in a medium mixing bowl and sprinkle the sugar and salt over it. Grate the lemon rind directly into the bowl so that no aromatic oils are lost. With a knife, cut the butter into small pieces, dropping them into the flour. Using your fingertips, work the butter and flour together until it resembles coarse meal. Add the egg yolks, mix well, and gather into a ball. Divide into portions for desired use and press the pastry into the baking pans. This amount will fill two 9-inch tart pans. Chill the pastry-lined pans 30 minutes to an hour, or freeze, tightly wrapped, until wanted.

If the pastry shells are to be filled and baked, prebake them at 450° for 15 minutes, until the shine has disappeared but before they brown. Cool on a rack. Fill and bake according to filling directions. If tarts will have an uncooked filling such as fresh berries, bake at 375° for 35 to 45 minutes until golden brown. Cool on a rack. Pastry may be stored in the refrigerator, well wrapped, for several days.

PEACH TART WITH NOUGAT TOPPING

YIELD: ONE 9-INCH TART OR 6 SERVINGS

1 SHELL SWEET TART PASTRY (PAGE 106)
3 TABLESPOONS HEAVY WHIPPING CREAM
3 TABLESPOONS UNSALTED BUTTER
3 TABLESPOONS MILD HONEY
3 TABLESPOONS SLICED UNBLANCHED ALMONDS
2½ CUPS SLICED AND PEELED PEACHES

Prepare the pastry according to recipe instructions and allow to cool while preparing the topping.

To prepare the topping, place the cream, butter, and honey in a medium saucepan and boil over medium heat, watching carefully, until light brown. Stir in the nuts and set aside. Preheat the oven to 375°.

To arrange the peaches in the tart shell, strew about one-third of the fruit in the bottom of the shell and arrange the rest in neat concentric circles on top. Spoon the nougat topping over the fruit. Bake until the fruit is tender and the juices bubble, 35 to 45 minutes. Cool.

Variation: *Apricots or nectarines may be substituted in this recipe. Apricots should be halved and placed cut side down very close together. They need not be peeled. Nectarines also need not be peeled unless you object to the slightly shriveled skins that result from baking.*

Italian Ricotta Tart

Pastries of cheese sweetened with honey like this one have been made since ancient Roman times. Using liqueurs for flavoring is rather like the practice of the ancient Greeks and Romans of heightening flavor by adding drops of perfume to their mixtures.

YIELD: ONE 9-INCH TART OR 8 SERVINGS

PASTRY

2 CUPS FLOUR

3 TABLESPOONS SUGAR

½ TEASPOON SALT

½ CUP PLUS 2 TABLESPOONS UNSALTED BUTTER, COLD

1 EGG YOLK

2 TABLESPOONS DRY SHERRY

FILLING

12 OUNCES RICOTTA CHEESE

2 TABLESPOONS HONEY

2 EGGS

2 TABLESPOONS CHOPPED CANDIED ORANGE PEEL (PAGE 54)

2 TABLESPOONS SLICED ALMONDS

2 TABLESPOONS PINE NUTS

1 TABLESPOON KIRSCH

1 TABLESPOON GRAND MARNIER

CONFECTIONERS' SUGAR FOR DUSTING

To prepare the pastry, sift the flour, sugar, and salt together into a mixing bowl. Cut the butter in large flakes into the flour. Add the egg yolk and mix together with your fingertips until well coated by flour. Sprinkle in sherry as needed until the dough adheres in a ball. Wrap the dough in waxed paper and refrigerate dough about an hour so it is easier to handle.

Roll out less than ¼-inch thick and fit into a 9-inch tart pan with a removable bottom. (Avoid stretching the pastry.) Build a small edge. Cut eight to ten strips ½-inch wide from a rectangle rolled out of the trimmings to make a lattice top. Chill the shell while mixing the filling. Preheat the oven to 375°.

To prepare the filling, sieve the ricotta into a mixing bowl. Add the honey, eggs, fruit peel, nuts, and liqueurs, mixing until smooth. Pour into the prepared shell and weave a lattice top with the strips of dough. Bake 45 minutes, until puffed and golden. Serve barely warm or cooled, dusted with the powdered sugar.

CHEESE TART WITH BERRIES

YIELD: ONE 9-INCH TART OR 6 SERVINGS

1 SHELL SWEET TART PASTRY (PAGE 106)
1 PINT FRESH BLUEBERRIES
2 TABLESPOONS PLUS 1 TEASPOON LIGHT HONEY
FRESHLY SQUEEZED LEMON JUICE
4 OUNCES CREAM CHEESE OR SIEVED RICOTTA CHEESE
¼ CUP HEAVY WHIPPING CREAM (APPROXIMATELY)
¼ TEASPOON VANILLA EXTRACT

Use one 9-inch tart shell that has been prebaked. Cool while preparing the filling.

Wash the blueberries and remove any stems or inferior berries. Place one-quarter of the berries in a small saucepan with 2 tablespoons of the honey and cook over medium heat until it makes a fairly thick jam. Remove from the heat, add lemon juice to taste. (Large cultivated berries tend to be sweet and may require a tablespoon; tiny sour berries may need no additional tartness.) Mix the warm jam through the uncooked berries and cool.

Place the cream cheese in a small, deep mixing bowl and begin whipping it, adding a thin stream of cream. Use only as much cream as needed to develop a nice spreading consistency. Add the remaining honey and the vanilla. Shortly before serving, spread the cheese in the cooled pastry crust and top with berries.

Variation: *Top the cheese mixture in the shell with neat rows of strawberries, hulled and placed stem side down. Boil 3 tablespoons currant jelly in a small pan until thickened and brush carefully over the berries to glaze them. The whipped cheese topping is delicious served with fruit for dessert. A little more cream can be used and the soft mixture spooned over bowls of strawberries. Or shape pastry for a 9-inch shell into smaller tartlets. This amount of dough will make eighteen 2-inch tartlets or five 4-inch round tartlets. Bake until golden brown, 12 to 15 minutes, depending on size.*

Rich Walnut Tart

A famous Swiss specialty, this walnut praline tart is elegant and fantastically rich. Serve it only in small wedges. For a delicious variation, spread the dough with raspberry jam before adding the nut filling.

YIELD: ONE 9-INCH PASTRY OR 12 SERVINGS

PASTRY
3 CUPS UNBLEACHED WHITE FLOUR
3 TABLESPOONS SUGAR
PINCH OF SALT
1 CUP UNSALTED BUTTER, COLD
1 EGG
1 TABLESPOON RUM
GRATED RIND OF 2 LEMONS

FILLING
1 CUP HEAVY WHIPPING CREAM
1¼ CUPS SUGAR
3 TABLESPOONS HONEY
2 TABLESPOONS KIRSCH
3 CUPS BROKEN WALNUTS

GLAZE
1 EGG YOLK
2 TABLESPOONS HEAVY WHIPPING CREAM

To prepare the dough, place the flour in a large mixing bowl and mix the sugar and salt through it. Cut the butter into large flakes, letting them drop into the flour. With your finger-tips, work the cold butter and flour together to make a coarse meal. Break the egg into a large measuring cup, add the rum. Grate the lemons directly into the bowl of dough so that no aromatic oils are lost. Add the egg mixture and toss all together with a fork until well combined. With your hands, work together into a firm ball. Chill at least 2 hours.

On a lightly floured surface, roll three-quarters of the dough ⅛-inch thick. Line a 9-inch springform pan with the pastry, fitting it in without stretching it to avoid later shrinkage. Chill the pastry-lined pan and reserved dough while preparing the filling.

To prepare the filling, scald the cream and set aside. Caramelize the sugar in a large dry skillet, stirring to keep the browning uniform. When the sugar is a caramel color, add the warm cream slowly, stirring constantly. When the mixture is smooth and evenly mixed, remove it from the heat and add the honey, kirsch, and walnuts. Pour into the prepared pan.

Preheat the oven to 350°. Roll out the remaining dough ⅛-inch thick and cut into eight or ten strips about 10 inches long. Use them to weave a lattice topping. Press the edges firmly to the edge of the tart shell. Mix together the egg yolk and cream and brush on all pastry surfaces. Bake 40 to 45 minutes, until golden brown. Cool in the pan.

GREEK MOLDED HONEY CHEESECAKE

The antecedent of this Greek dish, introduced into Russia during the days of the Byzantine Empire, was trans-
lated into pashka, a molded cheese embellished with candied fruits still being served in Russian homes at
Easter. Neither of these dishes, despite their names, are cheesecakes in the current sense of the word.

YIELD: 12 SERVINGS

1$\frac{1}{2}$ POUNDS RICOTTA CHEESE
2 TABLESPOONS HONEY
1 TABLESPOON SWEET WINE OR CREAM SHERRY
$\frac{1}{4}$ CUP GRATED ALMONDS (SEE NOTE)

Combine the cheese, honey, and wine, beating until well blended. Butter a 1-quart decorative mold and dust with some of the grated almonds. Add the rest of the almonds to the cheese mixture, blending thoroughly. Press the cheese into the mold firmly and evenly. Run a spatula across the cheese to smooth the surface. Cover and chill for 24 hours. To serve, dip the mold into hot water for a few seconds, then invert on a serving plate. Surround with fresh strawberries, peaches, or apricots. Cut into wedges and serve with a portion of fruit.

NOTE: Chop almonds, place in work bowl of a food processor, and process until a fine, dry meal is formed (1 to 2 minutes).

OTHER DESSERTS

HONEY-VANILLA CUSTARD

Because custard is an excellent carrier for honey flavor, the character of this dessert will change according to the specific honey you use. Clover, alfalfa, and orange blossom are good choices, but go ahead, try something different.

YIELD: 8 SERVINGS

4 EGGS
⅓ CUP HONEY, SLIGHTLY WARMED
2½ CUPS WHOLE MILK
¼ TEASPOON SALT
½ TEASPOON VANILLA EXTRACT
WHOLE NUTMEG

Preheat the oven to 325°. Butter eight custard cups and prepare a pan of hot water 1 inch deep to hold them. In a medium bowl, beat the eggs lightly and add the honey, milk, salt, and vanilla. Mix thoroughly. Strain and pour into the cups. Grate nutmeg onto the surface of each. Place the cups in the hot water bath and bake 40 minutes, or until the centers barely jiggle. Remove and cool slightly before serving, or chill thoroughly.

Brown Rice Pudding

YIELD: 6 TO 8 SERVINGS

1½ CUPS COOKED SHORT- OR LONG-GRAIN BROWN RICE
1 CUP WHOLE MILK
1 TABLESPOON UNSALTED BUTTER
½ CUP CHOPPED DRIED APRICOTS
2 EGGS
5 TABLESPOONS HONEY, LIGHT OR DARK
¼ TEASPOON SALT
½ TEASPOON VANILLA EXTRACT

Place the cooked rice in a saucepan, add ½ cup of water, and cook over medium heat until most of the water is absorbed. Add the milk and cook a few minutes longer. Remove from the heat and stir in the butter and apricots.

Preheat the oven to 325°. In a small bowl, beat the eggs with the honey, salt, and vanilla. Stir into the rice. Pour into a greased 1½-quart baking dish and set into a pan of hot water. Place in the oven and bake about 45 minutes, until only the center jiggles when the dish is gently moved. Good warm or cold.

BAKLAVA

Baklava is one of the world's top honey sweets: dozens of layers of phyllo dough filled with butter and walnuts and drenched in a spicy honey syrup. Frozen phyllo is available in many supermarkets and in Greek and Mediterranean groceries. Follow the package directions for handling.

YIELD: 16 PASTRIES

9 PHYLLO PASTRY SHEETS FROM A 1-POUND PACKAGE
1 GENEROUS CUP FINELY CHOPPED WALNUTS
$\frac{1}{2}$ CUP UNSALTED BUTTER, MELTED
ABOUT 1 CUP BASIC HONEY SYRUP FOR PASTRIES (PAGE 126)

Unroll the phyllo dough and place an 8-inch round cake pan on a stack of the sheets. Using the pan as a pattern, cut around it with a sharp knife to make pastry circles. Repeat the process to make another stack. On the remaining border of phyllo, cut a stack of semi-circles large enough to cover the bottom of the pan, overlapped. Butter the cake pan. Preheat the oven to 350°.

   Place one circle of dough on the bottom of the pan and brush with melted butter. Repeat for six layers. Sprinkle $\frac{1}{4}$ cup of the walnuts over this pastry base. Cover with a circle of dough, brush with butter and sprinkle with a scant tablespoon of walnuts. Repeat for fifteen layers. Once or twice as the stack grows, press it together firmly with your hands. Finish with six layers of phyllo only, brushing each with butter. Score $\frac{1}{2}$-inch deep with the tip of a sharp knife to mark sixteen triangular pieces. Bake for 45 minutes, until a rich golden brown. While the pastry is still hot, pour the cooled honey syrup over it. Slice through the remaining layers of phyllo and let cool in the pan several hours before serving.

Opposite page: Baklava (above), and Honey Ice Cream (page 123).

ARMENIAN FRUITED WHEAT PUDDING

Anoush abour is a favorite Armenian sweet associated with Christmas and other important occasions, such as the birth of a baby. Similar puddings are made in the Ukraine, where it is called kutia. A spoonful of kutia is tossed toward the ceiling; if it sticks, it is a sign that the bees will swarm and the next year's harvest will be bountiful.

YIELD: 8 GENEROUS SERVINGS

1 CUP WHOLE WHEAT BERRIES
¼ TEASPOON SALT, OR TO TASTE
⅓ CUP GOLDEN RAISINS
3 TABLESPOONS PINE NUTS
3 TABLESPOONS CHOPPED WALNUTS
3 TABLESPOONS BLANCHED ALMONDS, HALVED
10 DRIED APRICOTS, CUT INTO QUARTERS
2½ TABLESPOONS SUGAR
2½ TABLESPOONS HONEY
3 DROPS ROSE WATER
CINNAMON SUGAR, FOR GARNISH

Wash the wheat with boiling water and drain. Place in a heavy saucepan with water to cover and bring to a boil. Boil 2 minutes, then cover and set aside for 1 hour. Drain the soaked wheat, return to the saucepan, add 1¾ cups boiling water, cover, and simmer very slowly until the grain is tender, 4 hours or more. Check occasionally to see if more boiling water is needed. When the grain is nearly tender, add the salt cautiously, stirring in just enough to eliminate the bland, watery taste. The grain is done when the mixture resembles a thick porridge. Add the raisins, pine nuts, walnuts, almonds, apricots, sugar, honey, and rose water. Stir over low heat to dissolve the sugar, mixing thoroughly. Spoon into a serving bowl. Chill thoroughly. Serve with cinnamon sugar.

Hazelnut Honey Charlotte

YIELD: 6 SERVINGS

1 TABLESPOON UNFLAVORED GELATIN
2 TABLESPOONS COLD WATER
4 EGG YOLKS
¼ CUP SUGAR
¼ CUP HONEY
1 CUP MILK, HEATED TO THE BOIL WITH A 1-INCH VANILLA BEAN
12 TO 15 LADYFINGERS
1 CUP HEAVY WHIPPING CREAM, WHIPPED
½ CUP BLANCHED AND GRATED TOASTED HAZELNUTS

In a small container, dissolve the gelatin in the cold water. Place the container in a small pan of hot water until the mixture is clear and smooth. Beat together the egg yolks and sugar. Stir in the honey and add the milk slowly, stirring constantly with a wire whip. Heat gently in a small, heavy saucepan, whisking often, until thickened and smooth. Remove the vanilla bean. Add the gelatin mixture and set aside to cool, stirring occasionally to prevent a skin from forming.

Line a 1½-quart charlotte mold with the ladyfingers, trimming them so that the ladyfingers meet in the center in an attractive design. (Use trimmings to fill in any unmatched corners.) When the custard is cool but not firm, fold in the whipped cream and the hazelnuts. Pour into the prepared mold. Refrigerate until firm, several hours or overnight. Unmold and cut in wedges to serve.

Toasted Almond Pumpkin Flan

YIELD: 8 SERVINGS

½ CUP SUGAR
¼ CUP HOT WATER
½ CUP CHOPPED BLANCHED ALMONDS
1 CUP UNSWEETENED PUMPKIN PURÉE
½ CUP HONEY
1½ CUPS (12-OUNCE CAN) EVAPORATED MILK
⅓ CUP WATER
½ TEASPOON SALT
1 TEASPOON GROUND CINNAMON
1½ TEASPOON VANILLA EXTRACT
5 EGGS, BEATEN

Prepare a pan of hot water large enough to hold a 1½-quart baking dish. Caramelize the sugar in a dry skillet over medium heat, watching closely and stirring as needed. When it has turned a rich golden brown, add ¼ cup hot water, stirring again until smooth. Cool slightly.

Preheat the oven to 325° and toast the almonds in a single layer in the oven for 10 minutes, until light brown. Stir them into the caramel and pour this mixture into the baking dish, tilting it to spread the caramel up the sides of the dish. Preheat the oven to 350°. In a medium bowl, mix together the purée, honey, milk, ⅓ cup of water, the salt, cinnamon, and vanilla. Add the eggs, blending them into the pumpkin mixture.

Pour the filling into the caramel-lined baking dish and set in the pan of hot water. Bake 70 minutes, or until only the center jiggles when pan is gently shaken. Cool, then refrigerate. Serve chilled, unmolding the flan onto a serving plate.

HONEY ICE CREAM

This ice cream, significantly lighter than the famous Alice B. Toklas formula for honey ice cream (which calls for 6 egg yolks), is sensational for its powerful flavor bouquet and smooth texture. Try substituting different kinds of honey to create distinctive flavors. Omit the orange rind and almond to emphasize the honey character.

YIELD: ABOUT 2 QUARTS

²⁄₃ CUP CHOPPED, BLANCHED ALMONDS
3½ CUPS HEAVY WHIPPING CREAM
²⁄₃ CUP HONEY
GRATED RIND OF 2 ORANGES
1 TEASPOON ALMOND EXTRACT
¼ TEASPOON SALT

Preheat the oven to 325°. Spread the almonds on a jelly-roll pan and toast for 10 to 15 minutes or until golden. Set aside. In a large mixing bowl, beat the cream until slightly thickened. Add the honey gradually, beating until the mixture is well blended. Stir in the orange rind, almond extract, and salt. Freeze in an ice cream maker, adding the nuts as the mixture begins to harden. Freeze until quite firm, then transfer to a covered container, and let mellow in the freezer compartment for a few hours before serving.

STEAMED CRANBERRY PUDDING

Serve this pudding hot in wedges, with Honeyed Brandy Butter (page 127) or Honey Lemon Sauce (page 128).

YIELD: 6 SERVINGS

1½ CUPS FLOUR
½ TEASPOON SALT
1 TEASPOON BAKING SODA
½ TEASPOON BAKING POWDER
2 CUPS FRESH CRANBERRIES
⅔ CUP HONEY
⅓ CUP HOT WATER
GRATED RIND OF 1 ORANGE
¼ TEASPOON GROUND DRIED GINGER
¼ CUP CHOPPED ALMONDS

Grease well a 1½-quart steamed-pudding mold. Sift the flour, salt, baking soda, and baking powder together. Stir in the cranberries, discarding any soft ones. Dilute the honey with the hot water and add the liquid to the dry ingredients, beating to make a smooth batter. Grate the orange rind directly into the bowl so that no aromatic oils are lost. Add the ginger and the nuts and stir well.

Pour into the prepared mold and fasten the cover tightly. The mold should be no more than two-thirds full, to allow for expansion. Place on a rack in a deep kettle and pour hot water halfway up the sides of the mold. Cover the kettle, bring to a boil, then decrease the heat to maintain a simmer for 2 hours while the pudding steams. Remove from the pan and cool in the mold a few minutes before turning out onto a serving plate.

SYRUPS
and
TOPPINGS

Basic Honey Syrup for Pastries

Mediterranean baked sweets are often soaked in honey syrup while still warm, then allowed to cool before serving. Because straight honey would be too sweet and viscous, it is diluted in a thin sugar syrup that is flavored with citrus and spices. Since honey syrup keeps well at room temperature, it can be made in large batches for storing in the pantry. This recipe gives proportions for 1 pound of honey. Dark Greek honey, the kind made from thyme and oregano, lends a wonderful complex flavor to a syrup, but you can use any honey.

YIELD: 1 QUART

2⅔ CUPS SUGAR

2 CUPS WATER

STRIPS OF RIND OF 1 SMALL LEMON

3 WHOLE CLOVES

3 CINNAMON STICKS

1 POUND HONEY, DARK

5 TABLESPOONS FRESHLY SQUEEZED LEMON JUICE

2½ TABLESPOONS BRANDY

Combine the sugar, water, lemon rind strips, cloves, and cinnamon sticks in a saucepan and bring to a boil. Decrease the heat and simmer until the syrup thickens slightly, 10 to 15 minutes. Strain out the rind and spices. Stir in the honey, lemon juice, and brandy. Cool. Store in clean jars and use as needed for Greek pastries.

Honeyed Brandy Butter

YIELD: ABOUT 1 CUP

½ CUP UNSALTED BUTTER
½ CUP HONEY
2 TABLESPOONS BRANDY OR RUM
FRESHLY GRATED NUTMEG

Cream the butter. Add the honey and blend thoroughly. Add the brandy, a few drops at a time, beating until the mixture is fluffy. Add nutmeg to taste, transfer to a crock or small bowl, and chill thoroughly. Serve on steamed cranberry pudding.

Honey Butter

Wonderful on toast, pancakes, waffles, biscuits, cornbread, or warm gingerbread.

YIELD: ABOUT ½ CUP

½ CUP UNSALTED BUTTER
¼ CUP HONEY

Cream the butter, add the honey, and whip until fluffy and smooth. Store in small covered crocks, refrigerated, up to a week.

Variations: *Add the grated rind of half an orange and blend well. Or add 1 tablespoon finely chopped toasted almonds or add ¼ teaspoon ground cinnamon.*

Honey Lemon Sauce

Serve warm with gingerbread, hot puddings, or apple pie.

YIELD: 6 SERVINGS

1 TABLESPOON POTATO STARCH
1 CUP COLD WATER
½ CUP HONEY (OR LESS, TO TASTE)
GRATED RIND AND JUICE OF 1 LEMON
1 TABLESPOON UNSALTED BUTTER

Dissolve the potato starch in the cold water. Place in a small saucepan and stir in the honey. Cook slowly until thickened and clear. Off the heat, grate the lemon rind directly into the pan so that no aromatic oils are lost, then squeeze the lemon and strain the juice into the sauce. Stir in butter.

Spice Honeyed Cream

Serve as a topping with pumpkin pie, fruit pies, and gingerbread.

YIELD: 8 SERVINGS

1 CUP HEAVY WHIPPING CREAM
2 TABLESPOONS HONEY
½ TEASPOON GROUND CINNAMON OR OTHER SPICES

Whip the cream until lightly thickened. Beat in the honey and cinnamon.

Honey Sources

BALLARD'S APIARY
192 Vic Edwards Road
Sarasota, Florida 34240
Phone: (941) 371-7873; Fax: (941) 371-7288

Beekeepers, pollinators, and packers of raw honey from Florida sources, including orange blossom, tupelo, and palmetto. Also propolis, pollen, and royal jelly. Distribution in stores nationwide; will mail order.

BEE'S KNEES HONEY FACTORY
520 S.W. Yamhill Street, RG #2
Portland, Oregon 97204
Phone: (503) 225-0755; Fax: (503) 225-0216

Packers of American honey including alfalfa, blackberry, buckwheat, sweet clover, fireweed, holly, mint, orange blossom, raspberry, sage, snowberry, star thistle, thistle. Widely distributed through west coast stores; mail order.

BEEHIVE BOTANICALS
16297 W. Nursery Road
Hayward, Wisconsin 54843
Phone: (715) 634-4274; Fax: (715) 634-352
Email: beehive@win.bright.net

Packers of an extensive list of honey products including propolis, pollen, and raw wildflower honey. Distributed in stores; mail order.

BELLEVILLE HONEY COMPANY
18898 Dahlstedt Road
Burlington, Washington 98233
Phone: (360) 757-1073

Packers of honey in upper Washington state, including blackberry, fireweed, and raspberry. In stores and farmers' markets; will mail order.

CHAMPLAIN VALLEY APIARIES
Box 127, Middlebury, Vermont 05753
Toll-free: (800) 841-7334; Phone: (802) 388-7724
Fax: (802) 388-1653

Producer/packer of clover-alfalfa blend, unheated or liquid. Will mail order.

DEAN & DELUCA
560 Broadway
New York, New York 10012
New York store: Toll-free: (800) 999-0306, Ext. 269

Retail stores in several locations. Customer service will mail order; ask for a specific honey from their extensive selection of international and domestic honeys.

DRAEGER'S MARKETPLACE
222 East Fourth Avenue
San Mateo, California 94401
Phone: (650) 685-3700
Web site: www.draegers.com

Retail stores on the San Francisco Peninsula with a large selection of honeys from premium international sources and local suppliers. Will mail order.

DRAPER'S SUPER BEE APIARIES
RR 1, Box 97
Millerton, Pennsylvania 16936
Toll-free: (800) 233-4273; Fax: (570) 537-2727
Web site: www.draperbee.com

Producer/packer of American honey—their own, local beekeepers, and others. Alfalfa, basswood, buckwheat, clover, goldenrod, orange blossom, sourwood, tulip poplar, tupelo, wildflower; also comb. Beeswax, propolis, pollen, beekeeping supplies, and videos. In stores; will mail order; ship worldwide.

DUTCH GOLD HONEY
2220 Dutch Gold Drive
Lancaster, Pennsylvania 17601
Phone: (717) 393-1716; Fax: (717) 393-8687

Packer of American honey, wholesale and retail. Alfalfa, avocado, blueberry, buckwheat, clover, orange blossom, safflower, sage, tupelo, wildflower. In stores, especially on the East Coast; will mail order.

A. G. FERRARI
PO Box 1933
San Leandro, California 94577
Toll-free: (877) 878-2783
Web site: www.agferrari.com

Retail stores in the San Francisco Bay Area; honey from Italian artisan producers Daniel DeValle and Giuseppe Coniglio. Will mail order.

FORMAGGIO KITCHEN
244 Huron Avenue
Cambridge MA 02138
Phone: (617) 354-4750

Retail store with catalog; will mail order. Fine Italian honey from artisan producer Mario Bianco; Spanish lavender and rosemary; other fine international honey.

FORTNUM & MASON
181 Piccadilly
London W1A 1ER, England
Phone: (011) 44 171 465 8666
Fax: (011) 44 171 437 3278

Superlative grocer in London, with outstanding selection of British honey and honeys of the world. Will mail order. Shipping is efficient and fast, though costly.

FRUITWOOD ORCHARDS HONEY INC.
419 Elk Road
Monroeville, New Jersey 08343
Phone: (856) 881-7748; Fax: (856) 863-8104
Email: fruitwood@erols.com

Apiary and pollinators; about 2000 colonies. They produce blueberry, pine barren, cranberry, and spring wildflower, and buy from other beekeepers around the country. Crystallized honey and comb. Farmstand at their address; also in East Coast stores; will mail order.

GIBBONS BEE FARM
314 Quinnmoor
Ballwin, Missouri 63011
Phone: (314) 394-5395; Fax: (314) 256-0303
Email: SGIBBs314@aol.com

Artisan producer Sharon Gibbons. Clover and Ozark wildflower honey; fruit and honey spreads. In stores, farmers' markets; will mail order.

HAWAIIAN HONEY HOUSE
PO Box 430
Papaikou, Hawaii 96781
Phone: (808) 964-5401; Fax: (808) 964-5401
Email: hihoney@ilhawaii.net
Web site: www.alohamall.com/hamakua/hihoney.htm

Artisan producer Walter Patton. Christmas berry, lehua, macadamia, and tropical flower. In stores in Hawaii; mail order.

HONEY GARDENS APIARIES
641 Richmond Road
Hinesburg, Vermont 05461
Phone: (802) 482-5887; Fax: (802) 482-5882
Email: honeygar@sover.net

Artisan producer Todd Hardie. Northeastern wildflower, unprocessed; also comb. In local stores; will mail order.

JOANN'S HONEY
3164 Maple Court
Reedsport, Oregon 97467
Phone: (503) 271-4726; Fax: (503) 271-4726

Artisan producer Joann Olstrom; packer of local

Oregon honey. Blackberry, raspberry, foxglove and wildflower, Umpquah Valley wildflower, meadowfoam, pumpkin. In stores; will mail order.

KALLAS HONEY FARM
6270 North Sunny Point Road
Milwaukee, Wisconsin 53217
Toll-free: (800) 373-4669; Phone: (414) 964-3810
Fax: (414) 964-3809; Email: Kallashoney@aol.com

Packer of Wisconsin honey. Alfalfa, buckwheat, clover, cranberry blossom, orange blossom, sunflower, and wildflower. Also beeswax and pollen. In health food stores and others; will mail order.

KOST FAMILY APIARY
1408 Bunce Road
Frewsburg, New York 14738
Phone: (716) 569-3148
E-mail: buzzme@madbbs.com

Artisan producers Sandy Ivy and John Kost; about 100 colonies. Basswood, spring tree blossom, black locust, goldenrod blend; comb. In stores; will mail order.

LANEY FAMILY HONEY COMPANY
25725 New Road
North Liberty, Indiana 46654
Phone: (219) 656-8701; Fax: (219) 656-8603
Web site: www.laneyhoney.com

Packer of Midwestern honey plus Florida orange. Basswood, blueberry, buckwheat, clover, cranberry blossom, Dune country, Michigan star thistle, wildflower, spring blossom, autumn wildflower; comb. In stores throughout the Midwest; will mail order.

MARSHALL'S FARM
PO Box 10880
Napa, California 94581
Toll-free: (800) 624-4637; Phone: (707) 224-6373
Fax: (707) 224-6388

Artisan producers Spencer and Helene Marshall place hives all around the San Francisco Bay Area and hand harvest them. Honey from many micro-climates. Sold at Bay Area farmers' markets and in stores; will mail order. Tastings at their Flying Bee ranch.

McLURE'S HONEY & MAPLE PRODUCTS
46 N. Littleton Road
Littleton, New Hampshire 03561
Phone: (603) 444-6246; Fax: (603) 444-6659
Email: maple@ncia.net

Packer of American honey. New York clover, Northeast wildflower, Florida orange blossom, Maine raspberry, Cape Cod cranberry; Honey in the Rough (raw with comb). In stores; will mail order.

MOON SHINE TRADING COMPANY
1250A Harter Avenue
Woodland, California 95776
Toll-free: (800) 678-1226; Fax: (530) 668-6061
Web site: www.moonshinetrading.com

Packer of gourmet honey. California yellow star thistle, orange blossom, eucalyptus, and black button sage; Hawaiian Christmas berry and lehua; Northwest fireweed; High plains sweet clover; Southwest desert garden; comb honey and flavored spreads. In gourmet stores nationwide; will mail order.

THE PASTA SHOP
5655 College Avenue
Oakland, California 94618
Phone: (510) 652-0462 or (510) 547-4005

Retail stores in Berkeley and Oakland. Fine honeys of the world; will mail order.

PETERSON HONEY COMPANY
9757 292nd Street
Chisago City, Minnesota 55013
Phone: (651) 257-1017; Fax: (651) 257-1017
Email: ktpeterson@stthomas.edu

Beekeeper Kevin Peterson, about 800 colonies; also makes honey wines. Minnesota clover, basswood, wildflower honey; Florida orange blossom. Sold locally in 12 stores; will mail order. Honey tasting as well as wine tasting at WineHaven Winery, same address.

PLAN BEE
PO Box 456
Salem, New York 12865
Phone: (518) 854-9239; Fax: (518) 854-9239
Email: infoplanbeehoney.com
Web site: www.planbeehoney.com

Artisan producers Mary Ehni and Stephen Fairley. Upstate New York wildflower—comb, liquid, and creamed; beautiful packaging; will mail order.

ROYAL PACIFIC FOODS
Monterey, California
Toll-free: (800) 551-5284

Will provide information on stores carrying Julian Wolthagen's Tasmanian leatherwood honey, or will ship direct if unavailable in your locale.

STOCKIN'S APIARIES
4 Reservoir Road
Strasburg, Pennsylvania 17579
Phone: (717) 687-7816; Fax: (717) 687-0283

Artisan producer Gary Stockin. Unprocessed local wildflower honey; liquid and comb. In stores locally; will mail order.

SUNNYLAND FARMS
PO Box 8200
Albany, Georgia 31706
Toll-free: (800) 999-2488
Web site: www.nutsandcandies.com

Pecan growers with a farmstore and catalog; also sell gallberry honey. Will mail order.

THISTLEDEW FARM
RD #1, Box 122
Proctor, West Virginia 26055
Phone: (304) 455-1728; Fax: (304) 455-1740
Web site: www.thistledewfarm.com

Artisan producers Ellie and Steve Conlon, about 600 colonies. Local floral blends. Also beeswax candles. In stores; will mail order.

VOLCANO ISLAND HONEY COMPANY
PO Box 1709
Honokaa, Hawaii 96727
Toll-free: (888) 663-6639
Fax: (808) 775-0412

Artisan producer Richard Spiegel. Rare white Hawaiian honey. In specialty stores nationally, including Neiman Marcus; will mail order.

ZINGERMAN'S
422 Detroit Street
Ann Arbor, Michigan 48104
Phone: (888) 636-8162; Fax: (734) 769-1260
Email: zing@chamber.ann-arbor.mi.us

Retail store with mail order department; ask for catalog with fine international varietal honeys, including Spanish rosemary, sunflower, and lavender.

For people who would like to know more about beekeeping, few resources are as valuable for the beginning hobbyist as a gathering of local beekeepers. In almost any part of the country, a county beekeepers' association can be located through your phone book or the agriculture department of a local university.

Another useful resource is Dadant & Sons, since 1851 a supplier of beekeeping equipment and publications, including *American Bee Journal*.

DADANT & SONS
51 S. Second Street
Hamilton, Illinois 62341
Phone: (217) 847-3342; Fax: (217) 847-3660
Email: dadant@dadant.com
Web site: www.dadant.com

Index

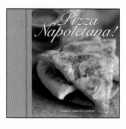